Playlist

"Last Goodbye"
Black Label Society

"If I Didn't Have You"
Thompson Square

"A Warrior's Call"
Volbeat

"Rearranged"
Limp Bizkit

"Boys 'Round Here"
Blake Shelton

"Lonely Day"
System of a Down

"The Hockey Song"
Stompin' Tom Connors

"Tubthumping"
Chumbawamba

"Bad Company"
Five Finger Death Punch

"Simple Man"
Lynyrd Skynyrd

"Rockstar"
Nickelback

"Second Chance"
Shinedown

"The More I Drink"
Blake Shelton

"Detroit Son of a Bitch"
Dirty Americans

"Coming Down"
Five Finger Death Punch

"These Days"
Foo Fighters

"Chalk Outline"
Three Days Grace

"Blue Jeans and a Rosary"
Kid Rock

"Girls, Girls, Girls"
Mötley Crüe

"Like Jesus Does"
Eric Church

"Whatever"
Godsmack

"Better Than I Used to Be"
Tim McGraw

My Last Fight

My Last Fight

The True Story of a Hockey Rock Star

Darren McCarty

with Kevin Allen

TRIUMPH
BOOKS

Library of Congress Cataloging-in-Publication Data

McCarty, Darren.
  My last fight : the true story of a hockey rock star / Darren McCarty, Kevin Allen.
    pages cm
  ISBN 978-1-62937-045-3 (paperback)
  1. McCarty, Darren. 2. Hockey players—United States—Biography. 3. Recovering addicts—United States—Biography. I. Allen, Kevin. II. Title.
  GV848.5.M39A3 2013
  796.9620922—dc23
                                    2013030979

This book is available in quantity at special discounts for your group or organization. For further information, contact:

Triumph Books LLC
    814 North Franklin Street
    Chicago, Illinois 60610
    (312) 337–0747
    www.triumphbooks.com

Printed in U.S.A.

ISBN: 978-1-60078-885-7

Design by Patricia Frey

Interior photos courtesy of the author except pages ii, 60, 70, 128, 142, 167, 218, and 250 (Getty Images), and pages 82, 90, 92, 125, 152, 182 (AP Images).

Insert photos courtesy of the author except where otherwise noted.

When I played with Bob Probert, I called him "Goomba" and he called me "Mitzy." This book is dedicated to you, Goomba, from your Mitzy, because whether people know or don't know, on and off the ice you were always my hero. You're the only person I had known that had a bigger and softer heart than me, and I know that because you let me in it. I miss you every day and thank you for paving the path you did so that I could learn—right, wrong, or indifferent. You telling your story gave me the inspiration and confidence to tell mine with 100-percent, no-punches-pulled honesty.

*This book is my tribute to you and Dani. I love you,
Probie. I'll never stop fighting.*

—Mitzy

"Take this love, take this life, take this blood it will never die, it ain't our last goodbye"

—"Last Goodbye"
Black Label Society

Contents

Acknowledgments

I'd like to thank first my amazing friend Kevin Allen for his tireless work on this project with me. From enduring hundreds of hours on the phone with me and all of my stories—good, bad, and ugly—to the hours he spent in putting this together to get my story—my side: the raw and honest truth—out to the world. Who says 20 years of covering athletes doesn't make a journalist an expert? Thank you Kevin for never judging me and proving that I can trust a journalist.

See, journalists and athletes can be friends.

Thank you to the greatest owners in sports, Mr. and Mrs. Ilitch—thank you for not only supporting me in my hockey career but also for making me feel like part of your family. Thank you to the entire Ilitch family and the Ilitch organization. Thank you also to Ken King, Darryl Sutter, and the entire Calgary Flames organization for the opportunity they gave me.

Thank you to all of my teammates and coaches, medical staff, equipment staff, grey coats, and everyone at the Joe; if I had to list the names of all of you that helped build and maintain my career this acknowledgment would be longer than the book. A few personal thank-yous to Piet and Russ for keeping me in one piece and stitching me up as much as they could. To Pauly for always making sure I had skates, gloves, and a stick—any equipment, no matter what. And to Tcheka for always altering my gear to my comfort and for keeping the tradition and helping out my son.

To Al and Uncle Joe, who have been there since Day 1 for my kids during the games. To John Hahn, Todd Beamer, Jim Biermann, and the rest of the Red Wing marketing and advertising staff for having my back in various ways the last 20 years and still today. And especially to

EVERYONE in the belly of the Joe—I love you ALL and thank you. I appreciate you as you all know by the big bear hugs I suffocate you with every time I see you.

To those few friends who have been there for me all along, from when I was hoisting Lord Stanley over my head to being where I am today. I love you and thank you for your honest, unwavering, unconditional love for me no matter what—namely Tim and Kammy Drummond, Jim Tochet, Don Zanzibar, Brad "the Dogg" Thompson and his wife KK, Brandon and Melissa Bordeaux, Charlie Waters, and Sammy Raffoul. And to Kim and Dawn, thank you for being my Guardian ladies. Can't leave out my rock star friends from the amazing Meltdown—Al Sutton, Chris Pernacki, Eli, Chaz, Lamb, and Wooj, Billy Reedy, Vince Mattias, and everyone ever involved in Grinder. Thank you to the Dirty Americans and Mikey Eckstein; to Roman Glick from Jackyl; Brother Cane; Robbie Merrill from Godsmack; Johnny Diservio, Zakk Wilde, and all my Black Label Society brothers and crew. A special thank you goes to Kid Rock—thank you "Big Time Bobby" for the memories.

To the friends I have gathered along the way. My closest friend, who is like my big brother, Bad Back Blackjack Jack Sully Sullivan. Can't forget his wife Trixie, and Punkin, Cornhole, Crazy Steve, Big Bird, K-Dubbs, Moose (RIP), Bronson, and everyone else that hung with me in "the Blind." To JT, Karyn and Gianni Thomas, Ron Gemsheim, Officer Joe Morgan, and Brad Frey. A special thank you to Paul Andoni and all of my other friends from Shields—you know who you are.

To my little buddies Boogs and LJ. What a ride—thanks for the destruction, construction, endless nudity, crazy drunkenness, and endless fucking belly laughs. You are all integral people at an integral time in my life. Sheryl and I couldn't have made it through the wars without you.

This book is also in honor of the late and very great Janet Hildebrant, who showed me life is worth living. To her husband, Greg, and to my beautiful nieces, Jordan, Carly, and Ashley. Uncle DMac loves you.

Thank you all for loving me as Darren and not as No. 25. I love you.

To my beautiful and hysterical sisters, Denise and Leslie, who each think they're my favorite. I'll take it to the grave which one of you really is. Ha! Thank you for keeping your sister sane and with me. And to my nephew Jon, who served several tours of duty. I am so proud to be your uncle.

Thank you to all the people at Triumph Books for allowing me to tell my side of the story—finally.

Thank you to my stepchildren, Nachelle and Brenden, for letting me love you as your other dad and for loving me no matter what. I am so proud of how your mommy has raised you and for the adults you have become: non-judgmental adults who love me without conditions. Thank you for letting me have your mom, I hope I make you proud.

To Griffin, my son, my warrior, who has the toughest role in life having to follow in my footsteps. You are not your dad, you're much better. I couldn't be more proud of you. Whether you make it in hockey or not I know you will be an amazing success wherever the world takes you.

To my girls, your daddy loves you very much and I look forward to seeing you bloom into the young women you are becoming. Stay away from the hockey boys so Daddy doesn't have to use his gun.

To my ex-wife Cheryl, thank you for raising such great children. I hope one day you move past the bitterness and find happiness and appreciation.

And I saved the best for last.

To my wife Sheryl (with an S), you are my best friend, you literally resurrected me from the dead, you saved me. I owe you my life. You have sustained me. Sheryl walked into hell to save me and then she walked back though hell with me to get me out of there, and she never let go of my hand once. She was never afraid. Thank you for seeing my vision, for your acceptance and letting me know I don't have to be "that guy," and for helping me to know that I am good enough. You have taught me honesty. Thank you for loving me and all my baggage unconditionally and without judgment. You are the toughest person I know in this world. Thank you for enduring the torture my past and present brings to you. I wouldn't be here without you. Thank you for never leaving and showing me my first taste of true, pure love. Thank you for loving my children, and thank you for bringing yours into my life to love me. I love you from beyond my soul. You are the Dani to my Probie.

"Couldn't live without you, baby, I wouldn't want to, if you didn't love me so much, I'd never make it through, this life would kill me if I didn't have you"

—"If I Didn't Have You"
Thompson Square

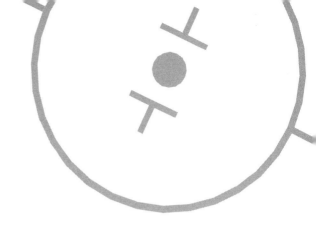

Introduction

"Let's Get Ready to Rumble"

—"A Warrior's Call"
Volbeat

Introduction

It feels as if my life is a Quentin Tarantino movie. My life feels fucking surreal. It's as if I'm one of Tarantino's characters, waking in a deadbeat motel with his life turned inside-out and left trying to figure out how he got there.

One day I'm a popular member of the Detroit Red Wings, making more than $2 million per season. The next day I'm living on an NHL pension and signing autographs to pay my rent.

Watching a Tarantino movie is like pondering the universe. You don't know where it starts and where it ends. There is no A, B, C order to any of Tarantino's stories. You are never sure how all of the pieces fit together. That definitely describes my life. I'm really not sure whether I'm at the beginning or middle of my story. Sometimes I feel like I'm in a flashback. There have been moments when nothing seems real.

I swear that I have partied with every character from every Tarantino movie. John Travolta's Vincent Vega character would not have been out of place with my after-hours crew.

My townhouse in Michigan was certainly full of "Inglorious Basterds" the night four years ago that I fully realized that my life had gone to shit.

At that time, my routine consisted of going to the bar at noon, closing it down, inviting everyone back to my place to continue the party, and then repeating the process the next day.

Then I met a woman named Sheryl who helped me realize that the people I was hanging out with probably didn't have my best interests at heart.

One night, with my home full of my party friends, I grabbed a hockey stick from the corner and slammed it over a table, shattering the blade. I wanted everyone out of my house for good.

Call it a cleansing breath, a moment of clarity in an otherwise hazy existence.

One of the guys in my house was so scared he barricaded himself in a bedroom. He was so petrified that he refused to come out even to go the bathroom. He said later that he almost took a dump in a bedroom dresser because he thought I might kill him if he came out of the room. That's fear.

Don't start thinking for a minute that you are about to read a Hallmark Channel story about how I finally divorced myself from the bad people in my life and have stayed clean and sober since then. That's not my life. It's not that simple. The first step to surviving addiction is to surrender, to throw in the towel, to accept that addiction is too much for you to handle without help.

The problem is that I've spent much of my life in a role where surrender is not an option. I've been an NHL tough guy. NHL tough guys don't surrender. We don't admit we need help. Initially, addicts fight aggressively to keep drugs and alcohol. We won't let anyone tell us what to do. But once we do surrender to the idea that we have to fight against our addiction, no one is more determined to overcome it.

The mental makeup of an NHL enforcer can be both a strength and a weakness.

Being a professional athlete does not mean that your life is always rainbows and unicorns. I'm an addict. There are no fairytale endings to addiction. I'm still a work in progress. Since I committed completely to Sheryl on December 31, 2010, she has helped me regain some focus in my life.

Since I committed to her and she committeed to me that cold December night, I have never cheated on her. I'm proud to say that. Maybe that doesn't seem like something to brag about. That's the way you are supposed to behave when you love someone. The devoted husband is the person I want to be. It's not the person I was when I was an NHL player.

Cocaine was never my drug of choice. I'm a weed and alcohol guy. But if cocaine was around, I used it, primarily as a means to sober up after being drunk. I called cocaine "the equalizer."

Those admissions should convince you that I don't pull any punches in this book.

Since the start of 2011, I have made strides in my recovery. At that point, I was drinking a minimum of a fifth of Jack Daniels every day, along with several shots of Jager, and 15 to 20 beers. I also was dabbling in cocaine.

In the late summer of 2013, I'm still drinking, but only beer. I never touch hard liquor. I smoke marijuana legally. I have a medical card that allows me to use it because of the constant pain I have from my hockey injuries. I have severe arthritis in my hands and shoulder from all of the fighting I did. I'm not looking for sympathy. I'm just giving you the facts.

Right now I'm a functioning alcoholic. I want to stop drinking. I believe I can do it. And there is evidence to show that I can do it. I went a decade without touching a drop. But I'm not sober today, and I may not be sober tomorrow.

Because I played a physical game for 15 NHL seasons, my body is a high-mileage vehicle. My parts rattle, and I don't start as well. My hands, because of the fighting I've done, look like the hands of a monster. I'm in constant pain. But I never ask for pain pills because I know where pill-taking will lead me.

This book is called *My Last Fight* because that's how I view my substance abuse addiction. It's a battle that I want to win, and I have to win.

But it is a grueling, ugly battle. It's not one you want to watch. There is no one cheering me on from the stands as I fight this battle. It's just Sheryl and me dealing with my addiction every minute of every day. My darkness can be overwhelming. I can be a sad, sick drunk, a suicidal drunk. Sheryl limits me to six beers a day, and some days I sneak in more. This is the toughest battle I ever faced.

Maybe this book will be therapeutic because it offers me the opportunity to set the record straight about my life. There are plenty of stories and so-called information floating around about what happened to me during my career and after I retired. Most of it is untrue.

Some of you think you know my story, but you really don't. Forget about what you have heard because this is the real story. This is the raw, uncensored truth about my career and life. Since every bad decision leads to a great story, this book is full of great stories.

My hope is that this book entertains, enlightens, and clarifies what it's really like to live on the roller coaster that is my life. Every day I wake up trying to find my balance. Every day I wake up not knowing what to expect. Every day I wake up wondering how exactly I got to where I am.

"Beware of false knowledge,
it is more dangerous than ignorance."

—George Bernard Shaw

Chapter 1

Motivate Me

"Heavy is the head that wears the crown, I'd love to be the one to disappoint you when I don't fall down"

—"Rearranged"
Limp Bizkit

Motivate Me

When I was a teenager, the prospect of someday inheriting my stepfather's heating and cooling business terrified me more than any hockey opponent ever could.

"If you die and leave me that business," I would tell my dad, "I am going to sell it the next day."

As a youngster growing up in Leamington, Ontario, Canada, it was clear to me that I was never going to be happy in a traditional workplace environment. I watched my dad work up to 18 hours per day, and I knew it wasn't for me. I worked for him only to raise money for hockey camps. I hated the grind. I would have to do the jobs such as washing the truck, cleaning the equipment, or squeezing into crawl spaces to replace a non-working part. I did grunt work. I knew how to cut sheet metal when I was 10 years old.

"This must suck for you," my stepdad would say, "because you can't quit and you can't get fired."

I was not a model employee. I liked it when my stepfather assigned me to clean the shop because I knew I could sneak up to the attic and grab a nap for an hour. I hated it when I was on a job with the guys because there was nowhere to hide.

One of my primary motivations for wanting to make it as a National Hockey League player was to avoid working as hard as my stepfather did.

Because I had attention deficit hyperactivity disorder (ADHD), I craved stimulation. No matter what I was doing, I needed to go 100 miles per hour with my hair on fire. Whatever I was doing, I was going to do it with passion and hyper focus.

Sports were the perfect outlet for my intensity. I could have been the poster child for the old-school ways of a young Canadian boy from a small town rising up to become an NHL player.

Perhaps my generation was the last to earn our way by living and breathing competition every waking hour. There were no video games to distract us, no texting to pull us away from our games, and no money available to make our path easier.

My biological father, Doug Francottie, was a cop in Burnaby, British Columbia. But he wasn't around when I was growing up because he and my mother, Roberta, split up right after I was born. They had been high school sweethearts, but they didn't last even a year after I was born.

The first important male in my life was my grandfather, Bob Pritchard, called "Jigs" by everyone who knew him. He was a World War II Air Force veteran and an immigration officer who owned a couple of acres of land in the town of Woodslee, Ontario, population 200.

It was country living. He had an above-ground pool and a creek. The neighbors owned horses. It was the ideal setting for a five-year-old to begin his exploration of childhood.

I was four or five when my grandfather taught me to drive. The only businesses in Woodslee were a gas station and a mini-mart. But it had an American Legion hall, and my grandfather would take me with him when he went down there to shoot pool and see the boys.

Since it was only a couple of blocks between the American Legion and my grandfather's home, he would put me on his lap and let me steer the car as he worked the brakes and gas pedal.

It felt like I was really driving.

My grandfather was the king of pranks and the master of the card game, Rimoli. He also had the patience to watch sports with me at any time.

We were a typical small-town Canadian family in the 1970s. My grandmother was the matriarch of the family, and Sunday dinner was always at my grandparents' home. Holidays were also spent there. Never would there be fewer than 10 people for any dinner that my grandmother cooked. Scalloped potatoes were her specialty.

4

Sports were a staple in our family. I had two third cousins, Chad Cowan and Robbie McMurren, and we were always involved in one competition or another.

The real sports influence on me was a cousin, Shawn Roberts, who ended up playing Junior C hockey. He was five or six years older than me, and yet he would let me get involved in games with his friends.

We would play everything, including tackle football, hockey, and chicken-fighting in the pool, and his friends never gave me any consideration for my age. They even stuck me in net when we played hockey. They toughened me up. I was about 12 when I started to be able to get my licks in during our games. That's the age when I began to hold my own against older players.

It was actually Shawn who also gave me my first instructions on how to fight standing up.

My mother bought a mobile home and parked on the corner of my grandfather's property, and I assumed we would live there forever. I was wrong.

When I was five, a man named Craig McCarty made a service call to our home to fix our air conditioner. I remember I was playing hockey in our gravel driveway with a squished soda pop can and a tree branch when he drove up. He asked my mother out, a romance followed, and on April 29, 1977, they were married. We moved to Leamington, Ontario, but my grandparents' Woodslee home still seemed like it was the center of my universe.

It was my grandfather who taught me how to fire a gun. It was my grandfather who held me accountable.

Craig McCarty was a good, hard-working man, but he didn't have the patience for a hyperactive youngster. We butted heads frequently when I was young.

But it wasn't an overwhelming issue because I kept myself busy.

I played every sport, and I excelled at every sport. I lived for sports. I was the kid who cried when his baseball game was rained out. I lived at the rink, skating whenever I could get on the ice. I played on my own team and with any other team that would hand me a jersey.

To this day, I believe that a child with enough talent to dream of playing in the NHL should still play another sport. When you are young, you need a break from your primary focus. My second sport was baseball. In that era, our Leamington area happened to be rich with good, young athletes.

By the time I was 12, I had won three All-Ontario championships. We didn't compete in the sanctioned international Little League tournament, but if we had I'm convinced that we would have represented Canada at the Little League World Series in Williamsport, Pennsylvania. I'm very confident in that belief.

When I was 12, we gave up four runs in the top of the first in the Ontario championship game and then won 23–4. I recall we only lost four games that summer, and we played in a multitude of tournaments.

Our top pitcher was Matt Derksen, and he could throw 87 miles per hour when he was 12. I was his catcher, and he broke my thumb three times.

We had another player on the team named Jason Wuerch, who ended up playing minor league baseball for years.

I was a decent catcher. When I was a 12-year-old, pitchers couldn't throw a fastball past me. I had good bat speed. I could have connected on a 100-mph fastball. My problem was the off-speed pitches. I couldn't hit the junk.

Derksen and I were great friends. His father owned a farm, and he would pay us 50 cents a bushel to pick tomatoes. The problem was that we often used those tomatoes to perfect our throwing motion.

At the end of the day, the nose-to-the-grindstone Mennonite tomato pickers would have 300 bushels and we would have 50.

Derksen was a big kid, and he was also a good hockey player. But as we all got a little bigger he seemed to lose his advantage and his interest. He was a farm boy who didn't want to leave home. He ended up marrying the girl he was with since he was about 14, and they have a very nice life.

My devotion to the sport of hockey probably started at age 10, when I convinced my stepfather to drop me off every morning at 6:00 AM so I could skate and work on my shot for an hour before school.

From the ages of six to 16, I went to the Can-Am hockey school every summer at the University of Guelph with the hope of continuing to improve my game. My parents would pay $400 for one week of camp, and then I would work for my dad to raise an additional $400 for a second week. My dad paid me $4 per hour, and it seemed to take me a fucking eternity to pay for that second week.

At 15, I scored about 80 goals playing major bantam hockey for the Leamington Raiders and it was time for my family to make a decision about my future. It was not an easy decision.

Brian Drumm had been named coach of the Peterborough Roadrunners Junior B team, and he told my parents he thought he could help me reach my potential if they allowed me to play for him. My parents were not jumping up and down with delight.

It was a big jump from major bantam to Junior B, and it was a rougher brand of hockey. The Roadrunners hadn't won a single game the season before and Coach Drumm was building the team from scratch.

However, the biggest issue was that Peterborough was 293 miles from Leamington, roughly a five-hour drive for my parents to visit and watch me play. It's an accepted Canadian tradition that top teenage hockey players must leave home to play at a higher level, but it doesn't mean Canadian parents arrive at that conclusion without some concern. It's never a slam-dunk decision to turn your children over to someone else to parent at an age when their decision-making impacts their entire life.

Coach Drumm said he believed he could work with me individually, and provide me with an opportunity to at least think about a career as an NHL player. He said I could live with him, and that he would make sure that I gave school the same attention I gave hockey.

This wasn't an easy decision for my parents. I can remember my stepfather, mother, and younger sister Melissa all sitting around the table discussing the pros and cons of me moving away from home.

All I could see was that playing junior hockey gave me the best opportunity to be the NHL player that I dreamed of being.

My parents could see the potential problems associated with a teenager living away from home without parental support. My stepfather's main argument was that the odds of me making the NHL were not in my favor. He made it clear that I was a long shot.

But my parents reluctantly decided to let me go, because both of them said they didn't want to stand in the way of my dreams.

My stepfather always said that you should never put yourself in a position to say, "What if …" That's why I've always been balls-out in everything I've tried.

They showed their support for my junior career by buying a cottage 20 minutes outside Peterborough. That made it easier for them to visit me every weekend. It was a strain on the family budget, but they felt like it was their commitment to my junior career.

However, as you could expect, Craig's belief that I didn't have much of a chance bothered me for a very long time. Nobody wants to be told that they have no chance to live their dream. As a human being, the ability to reach for the stars is what gets us through every day. If you have no hope, you have no life.

What Drumm told me was that in my first year I needed to establish myself as a physical presence and then work on my skills. He was the first person to tell me that he believed I could play in the NHL. Skating was always my issue. I didn't have a smooth, graceful stride. But I worked and worked at my skating. I went to Laura Stamm skating schools every summer. I would go down to the rink and skate for hours at a time, but skating remained the weakest aspect of my game. The description of my choppy skating stride at that time in my life was that it always looked like I was running on my skates.

My mom's worst fears about this new level of hockey were realized when she came to training camp in Peterborough and watched me pound the shit out of one of the team's toughest players in a scrimmage game. As my coach had recommended, I was simply trying to establish myself as a tough guy.

But my mom was furious. She would not even speak to me. That's not how I played as a bantam player. As a bantam, I played like Alexander Ovechkin plays today, driving to the net like I was a Humvee. I was a scorer, not a fighter. It was difficult for her to accept my new playing style.

In Peterborough, I was going to the same high school as the players who were playing major junior for the Peterborough Petes. Coached by Dick Todd, the Petes won the Ontario Hockey League championship that season. Future NHL players Tie Domi and Mike Ricci were both on that team, along with Corey Foster. Another prime scorer was Ross Wilson, who ended up having a lengthy minor league career. My lab partner in chemistry at the Peterborough high school was Jassen Cullimore, who was a 15-year-old on the Peterborough squad. He ended up enjoying a lengthy NHL career.

In addition to being a strong hockey player, Cullimore was a super smart individual. I'm still pissed that I failed chemistry because I didn't cheat off him as much as I should have.

In my one season with the Roadrunners, I established that I was OHL draft–worthy. In 34 games at the Junior B level, I had 18 goals and 35 points and enough fights to prove I could handle myself.

We were swept by Kingston in the opening round of the playoffs, but in the final game of the season I squared off against the team's tough guy. Don't recall who it was, but I remember he had a beard. I would not have been surprised if he had a wife and kids in the stands. He was much bigger and stronger than I was. To me, he looked old.

I remember the fight because I was just trying to hang on, and I remember laughing at the guy because I tied him up and he couldn't hit me. My grip on him was vice-like to the point that I fractured my wrist from the stress of just trying to hang onto the guy.

I also remember the fight because Drumm, dressed in cowboy boots, came off the bench to go after the guy I was fighting.

This kind of scene was not the kind of hockey my mother had bargained for when she agreed to allow me to go to Peterborough.

Now that I knew the Petes players and was familiar with Peterborough, what I wanted most was to be drafted by the Petes. Peterborough owned two picks in the third round of the 1989 OHL draft, and I was convinced one of those picks would be used to select me.

When the Petes passed on me I was devastated. But the Belleville Bulls soon selected me, and then selected Jake Grimes. As back-to-back picks, we met on the stairs going up to meet our teams and we ended up becoming close friends for three years.

My three seasons at Belleville could not have worked out better. Future NHLer Scott Thornton was an established leader on the team, and I ran him into the boards in my first scrimmage as a Belleville Bull.

I could hear Thornton talking to his teammates. "Who is the crazy fucker out here?" Thornton said. "What the fuck is wrong with the kid?"

But he fought me, and I held my own. And he became a tremendous mentor for me in my first season.

Rob Pearson and Steve Bancroft were also on the team. My coach the first season in Belleville was Danny Flynn, and my coach in my second and third seasons was Larry Mavety, the former World Hockey Association defenseman.

He was the perfect coach for me because he was old school and liked rough-and-tumble hockey. He reminded me of an old western cowboy. I have a deep voice, but not as deep as Mavety's voice. He didn't take shit off anyone, including his players. He had rules, and if you violated his rules you paid a price for that.

That was an era when pro wrestling was popular, and I remember three of us were watching it just before our noon gameday skate. Because of our TV watching, we were literally three or four seconds late getting on the ice.

Mavety went in the dressing room and pulled the television out of the wall. Then he yelled at us as if we had committed a capital crime. In his eyes, we had. We had disrespected the game by being late for a team skate. He was my kind of coach.

Just as Coach Drumm had taught me, I established myself in that first season. As a 17-year-old, I had 12 goals, 15 assists, and 142 penalty minutes in my first season in the OHL. I fought enough to set a tone for future seasons. Intimidation is a huge aspect of junior hockey. Age and size make a difference, and the older players have the advantage. When you are a younger player, you wait for your time to take advantage of that. I knew my time was coming because I had fought against the toughest players in my "class."

In my second season with the Bulls, I produced 30 goals, 37 assists, and maybe 20 fights in 60 games. My penalty minute total rose to 151. But I had 23 goals at Christmas time, and only had seven in the second half of the season.

What I also remember about the 1991–92 season in Belleville was meeting up with Kris Draper for the first time. He was playing for the Ottawa 67's, and he had come back from the World Junior Championships like he was jet-propelled.

I remember thinking, *Who the hell is the guy wearing a gold choker chain who can skate 100 mph in blue blades?*

Little did I know that the guy was going to end up being such a close friend in our days together on the Red Wings. He owns up to the gold chain, but he swears he didn't have blue blades, even though that's how I remember him.

The 67's beat us in six games during the playoffs, but what I recall most about that series was a fight between Draper and Brent Gretzky. I always tell Draper it was like watching a pillow fight.

Here were these two skinny-ass centers trying to fight like they were heavyweights. I believe Drapes won the fight, although I would never admit that to him.

It was like two little rats clawing at each other. The battle started behind the net, and when the linesmen finally moved in the fight was at the red line. Although they had battled for close to 100 feet, neither player had a mark on his face. It was like they were hitting each other with whipped cream pies. I've always told Draper that he lost that fight.

"You may have beat us in the series," I always tell him, "but at least I didn't get beat up by Gretzky."

No one in the NHL played more aggressive against Wayne Gretzky than Draper, and I've always believed it was because I razzed him all the time about being hammered by Brent.

Brent Gretzky was a quality player, and if he came out in today's NHL he would have had a long career. He could skate and play the game like Wayne. He just wasn't very big. In 194 games in Belleville, Brent posted 84 goals and 166 assists for 250 points. It wasn't easy being the younger brother of Wayne Gretzky, but Brent handled it better than I would have.

Brent and I spent a lot of time together. He took me to his home in Brantford, Ontario, and it was like taking a trip to the holy land. Their basement was like a shrine to Wayne. All of Wayne's trophies were there, along with all of the game-used jerseys he had collected through the years. It's an amazing display. It's like going through the Hall of Fame with no glass separating you from the displays.

The other memorable trip with Brent involved going to Wayne's home in Southern California during the summer. Wayne was away at the Canada Cup, and his wife, Janet, was also gone for the start of the week. So Brent and I had the run of the mansion. The only people around were the cook, Janet's brother, Jerry, and security guards.

Brent and I went to several parties, and met an endless stream of celebrities. I ended up picking up a model at one of the parties. I brought her back to Wayne's place, and we got frisky in the hot tub and pool. What I didn't know was that security guards taped and watched my sessions with the model. When Janet came home later in the week, she wouldn't stop kidding me about it.

When Wayne saw me over the next few years, he would say, "I hope you had fun at my house."

Even if nothing had happened between me and the model, I still would have said that I had a great time at Wayne's house. Just being at breakfast at Wayne's table and having gorgeous Janet Jones show up every morning wearing her housecoat was enough for me to call it a great trip.

If you are having breakfast with Janet Jones, you know you have made it.

From 1987 through 1991, the NHL draft rules allowed 18- and 19-year-old players to be chosen only in the first three rounds of the draft. Once you turned 20, you could be drafted in any round.

As a 30-goal scorer, I had a chance to be drafted as a 19-year-old. Rollie Thompson was my agent at the time, and he had heard that the Buffalo Sabres were considering drafting me.

When it didn't happen, I switched agents, going with Newport Sports. I also made up my mind to become a monstrous force in my draft year.

In the summer, I committed to a training regimen of mountain biking and rollerblading. I was in the best physical shape of my career.

In my third season with Belleville, it was fucking comical how much room I would get when I had the puck. If I skated the puck over the blue line, I could skate with it to the faceoff dots before I had to shoot. No one wanted to get too close to me.

I was named OHL Player of the Year after I scored 55 goals in 65 games. I finished with 72 assists and 127 points. Gretzky had 121 points. How many players can say they outscored Gretzky in junior hockey?

My analysis of my fighting career in the OHL is that I only lost one fight. Certainly I had some draws. Defenseman Jeff Ricciardi of the Ottawa 67's and I had some memorable battles, and neither of us ever gave an inch. We just stood there and battled toe-to-toe. But I don't think he ever bested me.

Ryan VandenBussche was the most enthusiastic fighter that I faced in junior hockey. I would tie him up until he couldn't reach me, and then I would tee off on him. He took more punches from me than anyone else because he would never quit. Honestly, I would grow tired and bored of hitting him. "Dude," I would say, "are you done yet?"

The guy who beat me in a fight was Tony Iob, who started with Kingston and then ended up with the Sault Ste Marie Greyhounds. He was a lefty, and he pounded me pretty good when I was a rookie.

But two years later, we had a rematch and I beat him as savagely as he had pounded me. The reason I remember that fight so vividly is because my mother was sitting in the first row, pounding on the Plexiglas, urging me on during the scrap. By then she had accepted that this was the player I needed to be if I wanted to play in the NHL. She knew that fight was important to me, and she knew that winning that battle with Iob was more important than scoring another goal.

That game against the Greyhounds was also memorable because I netted a hat trick against goalie Kevin Hodson, who ended up being my NHL teammate in Detroit.

In Belleville, we had a Bulls head in the arena that lit up, mooed, and puffed smoke every time we scored a goal. We lit up Hodson for 10 goals that night and when we played together in Detroit he told me he still had flashbacks and nightmares about that "that damn bull's head with its eyes lighting up."

What I was trying to prove to NHL scouts is that I could be counted on to protect my teammates and to do all of the dirty work that a role player needs to perform at the NHL level.

When the Red Wings interviewed me before the 1992 NHL draft in Montreal, I remember Ken Holland asking me, "What are you willing to do to play in the NHL?"

I looked him in the eye, and said, "Whatever it takes. A lot of guys will say that, but I'm someone who will actually do whatever it takes."

What I said must have had an impact, because the Red Wings drafted me in the second round, 46th overall. Curtis Bowen of the Ottawa 67's was Detroit's first-round pick.

About 40 members of my family were at the draft to hear my name called. We held a party in our hotel room afterward, and I remember that my uncle Vic McMurren, and my two cousins, Chad and Robbie, volunteered to make a beer run when we were running short.

No one was concerned when they didn't come back for 30 minutes. We just figured they got lost. Even when they weren't back in 60 minutes we didn't panic. But when they were gone for 90 minutes, we sent out a search party. Finally, after two hours, they stumbled into the room to report that they had been stuck in the hotel elevator for the entire two hours.

Only then did we realize that the case of beer now contained only empties. The trio had downed the entire case while they were trapped.

We all decided to go out to eat, but Robbie passed out before we got out the door. It was quite a night.

The only irritating aspect of my junior career is that we never truly had a good enough team to make a long postseason run. We were in rebuilding mode throughout my OHL career.

In my first season in Belleville, we were 36–26–4 and then upset Kingston in seven games of the opening round of the OHL playoffs. But we never made another playoff run.

Just making the playoffs was like our championship, and we did that in my final two seasons.

We just weren't deep enough. In my final season in Belleville, I had the 127 points, Gretzky had 121, and Grimes had 113, plus defenseman Scott Boston had 13 goals and 71 assists for 84 points and Tony Cimmelaro had 39 goals and 83 points. But no one else on the team had more than 50 points.

Another good memory I have of my junior career is playing against Eric Lindros. He was like the LeBron James of the OHL. He just muscled his way into the scoring areas and it was difficult to stop him.

But I would say the Bulls punished him as much as anyone. We never connected on him the way Scott Stevens did in the NHL, but I remember we hit him all the time because he never had his head up.

He had never had to worry about anyone hitting him before he got to the OHL, and we made him pay for his bad habit.

My junior hockey career had prepared me well for my NHL career. But the downside of junior hockey is that you have the ability to live like a wild adult far too early.

You're away from home when you're 16, hanging around with 18- and 19-year-olds. You're away from your parents. You're with well-meaning coaches and billet families who try to supervise your life, but they don't know you as well as your parents do. It's easy to get away with more.

In my first year in Peterborough, I had my first fake ID. I was running around like crazy, drinking, smoking dope, and partying like a rock star. I was probably drinking four or five times per week when I was playing junior hockey.

The night before the OHL draft was prom night at my school, and I recall being wickedly hung over at the OHL draft.

Even though I was a decent student, I failed chemistry and got a 50 percent in math. When I came home, my parents made me go to summer school, taking a bus every day for 45 minutes to go from Leamington to Herman, to bring up my grades.

You can say that I would have been exposed to the same temptations if I'd been going to high school at home, but it isn't the same when you're away from home and missing classes because of road trips. The level of supervision just isn't the same.

I can remember regularly going over after school to watch NHL fight videos with buddies and smoke weed. Could I have gotten away with that had I been living at home?

Mavety had a team rule against players going to bars, but he knew we were all drinking together somewhere. Actually, Mavety's rule brought us together as a team because it meant we all became friends. Our team had great chemistry.

It's a strange situation when you're going to a high school and you're not from that community. There's tension between the local students and the interloping high school players.

When I enrolled in Quinte Secondary School in Belleville, I tried to be a normal student. I got involved in drama and I joined the rugby team when my hockey season was over. I was disappointed that I couldn't play football. I tried to do my work, even when I missed classes. I encouraged my Bulls teammates to do the same time.

But there is no question that I was a wild man off the ice during my junior days. I grew up quickly when I moved away from home. Probably too quickly.

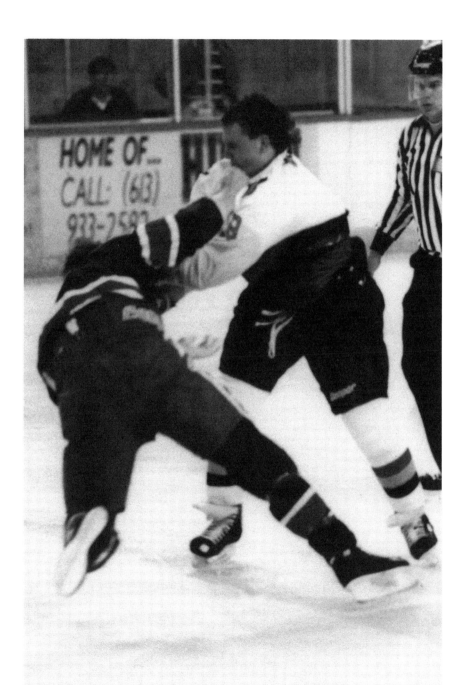

Chapter 2
The Apprenticeship

*"Talking 'bout girls, talking 'bout trucks, runnin'
them red dirt roads, out kicking up dust"*

—"Boys 'Round Here"
Blake Shelton

The Apprenticeship

When I played for the Adirondack Red Wings in 1992–93, we were the toughest team in professional hockey. I'm not talking about minor league hockey. I'm talking about pro hockey, including the NHL.

Eight players on that team boasted 100 or more penalty minutes. I put up 278 penalty minutes that season with only one misconduct penalty. My recollection is that I collected 45 fighting majors. Kirk Tomlinson had 224 minutes. Bob Boughner was at 190 minutes. Jim Cummins came in at 179. Dennis Vial was at 177. The late Marc Potvin had 109. Micah Aivazoff, one of our top goal scorers, even had 100. Serge Anglehart was probably the toughest guy on the team, but he didn't play much that season because of a bad shoulder. These guys all had NHL-caliber toughness.

Unquestionably, we tried to intimidate our opponents.

I vividly recall Tomlinson and I having Providence tough-guy Darren Banks cornered against the boards and arguing about who was going to fight him.

"I'm fighting him," I told Tomlinson

"Back off kid, I got him," Tomlinson replied.

Meanwhile, Banks is just standing there hoping one of us will fight him so he can go on with his life.

Before Tomlinson reacts, I jump in and start fighting Banks. Tomlinson was furious at me that I took his fight. We would argue all of the time on the bench about which opponent each would get to fight. There were not enough willing combatants to go around. It was a wild season.

My plan that season was to follow the same game plan Coach Drumm had given me when I played Junior B hockey in Peterborough. I had to establish myself to make people respect me. I fought every time I was given the opportunity. But I always felt as if opponents took it easy on me that season because they didn't want to face a murderer's row of tough guys if they hurt me.

Tomlinson would say, "Don't hurt the kid because if you do you know what will come next."

The art of fighting in pro hockey isn't as simple as the average fan thinks it is. There are unwritten rules that have to be followed. I learned that in my first NHL training camp when I beat up a guy in a rookie league game against the Toronto Maple Leafs.

On my way to the penalty box, I was high-fiving guys and celebrating like I had just won the championship belt.

Later that night, Red Wings assistant general manager Doug MacLean came up to me and said, "The way you acted after that fight is unacceptable. This is the NHL, not the World Wrestling Federation. A member of the Detroit Red Wings doesn't act the way you acted."

The message was received loud and clear. When it came to fighting, I wanted to do it the right way.

My willingness to drop the gloves against anyone, at any time, quickly made me a fan favorite. Fans seemed to like the fact that I chewed gum when I played. When I was done with a fight, I would blow a bubble just to show everyone I was fine. Fans sent me buckets upon buckets of Bazooka bubble gum. My dressing room stall was stacked three feet high with bubble gum.

Even though I was in the minors, I would have to say that season was among the most enjoyable of my hockey career. We had an incredible amount of fun that season. In addition to being tough, we could play. We were a skillful group. The season before, in 1991–92, Adirondack had captured the American Hockey League championship with Barry Melrose behind the bench.

The Los Angeles Kings had hired Melrose to be their head coach in the summer of 1992, and the Red Wings had brought in Newell Brown to be Adrirondack's new coach. He was only 30 years old, meaning he wasn't much older than some of the guys on the team. One of our goalies, Allan Bester, was 28. Ken Quinney and Bobby Dollas were two of our better players, and they were both 27.

The Adirondack team in 1992–93 was a mixture of veterans who thought they should be playing in the NHL, and bunch of younger guys such as Chris Osgood, Slava Kozlov, and me, who hoped to be there soon.

We had impressive offensive firepower on this team. Chris Tancill was like the Brett Hull of minor league hockey. He scored 59 goals in 68 games that season, and might have had an opportunity to take down Stefan Lebeau's league record of 70 goals had he not been recalled to the Red Wings for five weeks in the middle of the season.

One thing I will always remember about Tancill was that he was the speediest dresser I've ever seen. No one could don gear for a practice or game quicker than Tancill. He could dress cup to jersey in under two minutes. I know that because I actually timed him once because I was so fascinated by his dressing skill. He could walk in the door of the dressing room, and be out on the ice for practice in three minutes. It was one of the most amazing talents I ever witnessed in hockey.

Gary Shuchuk was another player who seemed like he should be in the show. He was a hard-nosed player, and he could dangle with the puck. Quinney and Mica Aivazoff were also 30-goal guys.

It was like an old-school team because all of the tougher players understood that our job was to make sure no one bothered our scorers. It was our job to make sure our scorers had plenty of room on the ice, and we did that job very well.

What made my Adirondack experience more enjoyable was the fact that the veterans considered it their job to make me a better hockey player. They wanted me to move forward in my career. The older tough guys made me their gofer to be sure, but they also sat me down and passed down the fighting wisdom they acquired. They taught me how to pick my spots to fight, and schooled me on the importance of timing my fights to help my team.

On some teams, the competition for playing time was a cutthroat endeavor, everyone looking out for themselves. But none of my Adirondack teammates were like that. They took me under their wing and said, "Hey, kid, we are going to help you get to the next level. You just need to pay attention to us."

About 15 of us lived in the same apartment complex. I was living with Boughner and Serge Anglehart. Chris Osgood and Mike Casselman lived together. Bobby Dollas and his wife lived in the same complex, as did Cummins and Vial.

It was a close-knit team. There wasn't much night life in Glen Falls, New York. So we made our own entertainment. We spent a lot of time together as a team. My keen interest in golf started because most of the players on my first pro teams were golfers. That spring, we played every chance we had.

At that time, I was just starting to break 100 and the older players, particularly Tomlinson, were established golfers. As I recall, Tomlinson was actually a Canadian pro. He gave me my first set of clubs.

Of course, the guys golfed for money and they weren't handing out handicap strokes to me. I either had to improve my game in a hurry or keep paying out money to these guys. I chose to improve.

One of the gambling games they played involved tying a red-and-white snake made out of tape onto the bag of the last guy to three-putt. Whomever had that snake on his bag at the end of round had to pay. I owned that fucking snake way too often. But it made me a better golfer. By the end of season I had probably shaved 10 or 12 strokes off my game. By the end of my first season, I could shoot in the 80s.

What I remember most about my first pro season is that we had many barbecues, drinking sessions, and plenty of adventures.

The Red Wings realized quickly that I liked to party too much, and general manager Jim Devellano suggested to my girlfriend, Cheryl, that she may want to consider moving to Glen Falls around Christmas that season. The Red Wings' hope was that she would tone down my act.

We moved into an apartment that was right above Osgood and Casselman's. What I remember most about that arrangement was that I was constantly downstairs playing Sega Genesis video games with Osgood and Casselman.

When we played that NHL game, I was always Chicago because the Jeremy Roenick player was God in that Sega game. Casselman was Washington and Ozzie was always Vancouver. We wrapped tape around a Gatorade jug and treated it like the Stanley Cup of video hockey. We wrote the winners of our tournaments on our Gatorade Cup. We would often play all night.

Sometimes, Cheryl would have to get out of bed and stomp on the floor to signal for me to come home.

When that would happen, Ozzie would say, "Your old lady is calling you."

It's the kind of shit you say when you are 20 and don't have a fucking care in the world. It was an awesome life.

That season was one adventure after another. Glens Falls is located in the mountains, and Gord Kruppke and Avisoff lived at the top of the mountain. We said they lived at the top of the world because it was a lengthy trek, on windy mountain roads, to get there.

But we would take advantage of that in the winter by attaching inner tubes to the back of Anglehart's truck. You would sit in the inner tubes and ski behind the truck as Serge flew around those mountain roads. There was nothing better than tubing at the top of the world. We always had the truck filled with players and girlfriends on our tubing expeditions.

One night I remember Stew Malgunas, Mike Sillinger, and I were on the tubes when the truck took a turn too sharply. We flipped over, and found ourselves sliding down the embankment. We tumbled about 20 feet until we were stopped by a well-placed tree. We weren't hurt, just pissed that our teammates had left us behind.

The guys in the truck didn't even initially realize we were missing, and they kept driving down the mountain.

"Now we have walk up this hill," Sillinger said.

"No, we don't," I said, and pulled a bottle of Southern Comfort out of my coat.

The three of us sat under the tree and drank most of the bottle while our buddies searched for us. We had some fun at their expense. We would yell to them, and then hide as they got closer. They had no idea whether we were injured or fucking with them.

Another time, I was on the tubes alongside Anglehart's girlfriend. She was about to slam into a garage on her tube and I made a dive off mine to knock her out of harm's way. The problem was that I ended up slamming into the garage and suffering a nasty hip pointer. I was a bruised mess.

When you are a professional athlete, particularly a first-year pro trying to prove you belong, the last thing you want to do is tell your coach you have been injured while tubing down mountain roads.

But my teammates had my back. The plan was that some of us would show up early for practice and go out on the ice. When Coach Brown showed up, everyone was going to say I had been hurt by crashing into the boards. My injuries were consistent with that kind of accident. The plan worked, I missed four games, and Brown had no idea what really happened.

My life as a pro hockey player was just as I hoped it would be when I was signed by the Red Wings.

I was 20 when I proposed to Cheryl. Most 20-year-old hockey players are not in a hurry to get married. Pro athletes at that age are far more interested in the promise of tomorrow than who might be by their side today. Her parents were like parents to me in Belleville; marrying Cheryl seemed like the right thing to do.

* * *

The 1992–93 Adirondack team deserved a better fate that season.

On January 29, 1993, the Red Wings traded Shuchuk, Potvin, and Jimmy Carson to Los Angeles in the deal that brought Paul Coffey to Detroit.

At the time that Shuchuk was dealt to Los Angeles he was leading the AHL with 77 points in 47 games. He had 24 goals and 53 assists. The Kings wanted Shuchuk because Melrose knew him well from the previous season in Adirondack when Shuchuk helped him win the title.

After Tancill was called up and Shuchuk was moved, we went into an offensive funk, highlighted by a stretch when we went 79 consecutive power play opportunities without scoring a goal.

At 14.69 percent efficiency, our power play ranked last in the AHL that season. But even for a team with a bad power play, Bentley University mathematics professor Richard Cleary says a slump of that magnitude would only happen once every 1,000 seasons.

For a team with an average power play, the chances of that happening would be once every 150,000 years.

Despite our power play woes, we still ended up as one of the top-scoring teams in the AHL that season. We finished with a 36–35–9 record, good enough for second in the Northern Division. The AHL was a highly competitive league in that era, evidenced by the fact that the coaches that season included names such as Barry Trotz, Robbie Ftorek, Marc Crawford, Mike O'Connell, Mike Eaves, John Van Boxmeer, and Doug Carpenter.

We expected to make some noise in the postseason. Tancill had been returned to Adirondack, and Sillinger had been sent down late in the season. He was a skilled offensive player. Kozlov, meanwhile, was improving daily.

We swept the Capital District Islanders in the first round, outscoring them 17–6.

The other good news was that Springfield had upset Northern Division–winner Providence in their first-round series. We were clearly the favorite in our second-round series. The Indians had a record of 25–41–14 during the season, and we had posted an 8–3–1 record against them in the regular season.

But the series against Springfield did not go as planned. We split two games in Glens Falls, and then split two games in Springfield. Tancill missed Game 4 because of the birth of his daughter, but he came back in Game 5 to record a hat trick, leading us to a 7–2 win. Finally, it seemed as if we were in control of the series. Again, that was not the case.

Before Game 6, Bester told coaches he couldn't play because he was having a marital issue. Bester's troubles were not the kind that gain you much sympathy in a professional dressing room.

Osgood stepped in and played well, but we lost a heartbreaking 2–1 game. Springfield's No. 1 goalie, George Maneluk, was injured during that game, but Corrie D'Alessio stepped in and played well to post his first win in about five months. With six seconds to go in that game, Sillinger believed he had scored the tying goal, but the referee said the puck never crossed the line. Sillinger insisted the puck had crossed the line, and D'Alessio had slyly pulled it back. Playoff hockey can also produce strange twists.

In Game 7, Maneluk and Bester were back in the net, and Bester didn't have a great night. We outshot Springfield 63–37 and lost 6–5 in overtime.

Kruppke scored with 1:15 left in regulation to give us a 5–4 lead, and we thought we were moving on in the playoffs. Then Springfield pulled Maneluk for a sixth attacker and Denis Chalifoux beat Bester with 51 seconds remaining.

We had outshot Springfield 17–5 in the third period. Maneluk, who never made it to the NHL, made 17 more saves in overtime. Then, Paul Cyr, a former NHL player on his way down, scored on a breakaway at 16:56 to win it for Springfield.

That series was probably one of the most frustrating stretches of my career. It didn't help that I couldn't buy a goal in that series.

It was not as if we didn't have our top guys going. Our top three forwards, Tancill, Aivazoff, and Quinney, had 39 points in 11 games. Sillinger was dominant with five goals and 13 assists for 18 points in 11 games. Dollas had 11 points in 11 games. He might have been the top defenseman in minor league hockey that season. In the regular season, he had seven goals and 36 assists for 43 points in 64 games. He also boasted a plus-minus of plus-54.

Even with the loss of Shuchuk, we should have had enough jam left to make a longer run in the playoffs. It was a very disappointing finish for all involved. We just couldn't keep the puck out of our net.

The only solace I took from the season was the fact that I had shown enough to prove that I belonged in the NHL.

I went into the next training camp believing I would make the team. The Red Wings had made significant changes after losing to the Toronto Maple Leafs on Nikolai Borschevsky's overtime goal in a Game 7. Bryan Murray stayed as Detroit's general manager, but he lost his place behind the bench. Scotty Bowman was brought in to get the job done.

Right away, it seemed as if Scotty liked what I could offer. In my mind, I made the team because of a fight I had at Chicago Stadium in a preseason game. It was against Cam Russell, and it's available on YouTube for those who care to see it first-hand.

The play started with Tony Horacek and Keith Primeau mixing it up in the corner, and Russell came flying in to help. I grabbed him and hit him a couple of times and put him down on the ice.

"You fucking jumped me," Russell bitched at me as I held him down.

"You want to go again? I'll go again," I said. "Let's go to center ice."

That's the way we did it in junior hockey, so I thought that was the way it should be done in the NHL.

We only made it as far as the blue line and then we started throwing punches. It was a great fight. It was like Rocky Balboa and Apollo Creed trading punches. He hit me, cutting me for five stitches, and then I buckled him twice with punches. He went down, and the crowd was going nuts. It was an unbelievable feeling to hear all of the fans cheering and yelling. That's what it must have been like when gladiators fought centuries ago. It was quite an adrenaline rush.

In the old Chicago Stadium, you had to walk down stairs in your skates to get to the dressing room. As I made the descent, fans were pouring drinks on me and showering me with popcorn and empty cups. I loved it, and I remember thinking that Bowman had to know that night that I was a tough competitor.

When I entered the dressing room, Bob Probert, who wasn't dressed for that game, was working out on the stationary bike. He looked up at me, and said, "Kid, you are fucking crazy."

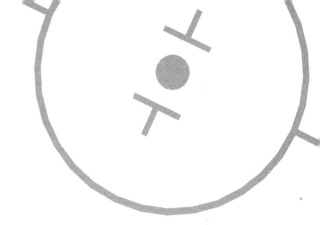

Chapter 3

Probie's Shadow

"Such a lonely day, and it's mine, the most loneliest day of my life"

—"Lonely Day"
System of a Down

Probie's Shadow

When I dreamed of playing in the National Hockey League, it wasn't about becoming the league's heavyweight champion. I admired Bob Probert, but I didn't want to be him. My objective was to play like Rick Tocchet.

I wanted to be a goal scorer who could fight, not a fighter who could score.

When I was playing junior hockey, Tocchet was my guy because the Philadelphia Flyers right wing could score 30-plus goals and rack up 200 penalty minutes like he was born to do it.

Once I scored 55 goals for Belleville I believed I had a shot to have the same impact for the Red Wings that Tocchet had for the Flyers.

I didn't want to be the Red Wings' heavyweight. I wanted to be the light heavyweight who fought on the undercard. I didn't want to be Batman. I wanted to be Robin, minus the tights. Although I was willing to fight anyone in the league, I had enough feelings of self-preservation to know that I didn't want to be in the heavyweight division.

Probie could play the game and fight, but once he established himself as the toughest guy in the league it became difficult for him to find a balance between his role as an enforcer and his offensive ability. It's easier to find that balance if you're a light heavyweight.

When I made the Red Wings team in 1993–94, I had the perfect situation because Probie was still on the roster and he was still king. In my rookie season, I fought 23 times and Probert only logged 15 fighting majors. But there was no question, he was still Batman and I was the Boy Wonder.

Again, I was following the Brian Drumm recipe to break into a new league: I fought often enough to establish myself as a tough competitor who wouldn't back down from anyone. By doing that, I bought myself enough room to be an offensive player.

With Probie in the lineup—and he played in 66 games that season—I had no pressure to fight the heavyweights. The NHL fight world is a different game when you are not obliged to fight heavyweights. If you are fighting in the heavyweight class, you are going to end up dancing with some guys who could end your career with a single punch.

I learned quickly that the tough guys I wanted to avoid were Tony Twist of the St. Louis Blues and Joey Kocur of the New York Rangers.

In my first NHL season, I ended up fighting Kocur in Joe Louis Arena and one of his punches cracked my helmet. The momentum of his fist connecting with my head sent us both crashing to the ice. We were both tangled up, and we went down head first and we landed face-to-face.

"You alright, kid?" Kocur asked.

"Thanks for not killing me, Mr. Kocur," I said.

In a not-so-surprising twist, one of my early NHL fights was against Dean Chynoweth, my frequent sparring partner in the AHL. It would have been funny if not for the fact that Chynoweth punched me in the helmet and caused a compression cut that required 40 stitches to close.

I had no idea that I was cut until I felt blood streaming down the side of my head.

As a fighter, I was never going to go down. I could take whatever you had to throw at me. But I'm a bleeder. I have a cement head and paper-thin skin. If I got caught with a punch, I was going to bleed.

My propensity to bleed didn't discourage me from enjoying my work. I enjoyed the physical aspects of my job. It fit my personality. I like to go balls out no matter what I'm doing, and that trait serves you well when you're in an NHL fight.

It always felt as if hockey fights were in my blood. It was part of my heritage. When I was growing up in Leamington it was already established that Essex County, or what some might call the Windsor area, was the cradle of NHL toughness.

Probert and Tie Domi of Belle River were well-established enforcers when I was playing junior hockey. Warren Rychel was born in Tecumseh.

The late Barry Potomski was born and raised in Windsor.

Ken Daneyko was not a big-time fighter, but he was a rough-and-tumble defenseman. He grew up in Windsor. Former gritty NHL defenseman Bob Boughner is also from the area.

It's like Essex County had its own fight club. Potomski had his first NHL fight in his second NHL game. Boughner picked up a game misconduct in his first NHL game and fought Eric Lindros in his third game.

My first NHL fight was against Bob Rouse, and it was in my fifth NHL game.

You have to fight in your first five NHL games if you want to be in the Essex County NHL Fight Club.

When people have asked me through the years why the Windsor area produced so many tough guys, I've said it was the water or those "meaty Leamington tomatoes."

But there were probably two main reasons why so many tough guys came from one area. First, every young Windsor-area player growing up in the 1980s idolized Probert. He was a very popular player in Detroit.

Second, the Windsor area is very much a blue-collar community and you grow up expecting to get your hands dirty to make a living. You grow up believing you will have to work for everything you have and nothing will ever come easily.

The area around Windsor doesn't produce finesse players. It produces old-school players with work ethics and a willingness to do whatever it takes to help their team.

In my first NHL season I fought Kelly Buchberger and Cam Russell twice, and also squared off against Kocur, Shawn Cronin, Donald Brashear, Basil McRae, Derian Hatcher, and Randy McKay, among others.

I have always believed that my fighting career was helped by the respect I had for NHL officials. My uncle Vic McMurren had been a Junior C referee, and when I was kid I spent a lot of time hanging out with referees. I knew they loved the sport as much as I did. NHL referee Dan O'Halloran was from my area, and I knew him as a family friend.

When I played in the NHL, I never lost sight of the truth that linesmen can save your ass if you are in trouble in a fight.

Do you think they don't remember who treats them with respect? I would disagree with a call that an official made, but I never disrespected them.

"I don't think you got that one right," I would say, and leave it at that.

Despite all of the grief that fans heap on them, I always felt that NHL officials got it right the vast majority of the time. I always tried to remember that they had a thankless job.

It seemed like Scotty Bowman liked what I could offer the team. I contributed nine goals and 181 penalty minutes, in addition to scoring two goals and adding two assists in the playoffs.

The only person who intimidated me that season was a U.S. immigration officer at the Detroit-Windsor Tunnel. I don't know her name, but I remember her name tag read: M. Brown.

Cheryl and I were to be married the following summer, but she lived with me in Novi.

My worry over what the immigration folks would say about Cheryl prompted me to go to the Red Wings officials and ask what I should do when Cheryl and I would go back-and-forth across the border to see our parents. They supplied us with a letter that explained that I was employed by the Red Wings and that Cheryl was my fiancée.

That worked well until we pulled up one night about 10:00 PM, when M. Brown was on duty. We'd been visiting my relatives.

I pulled out the letter and she told me the letter didn't mean anything legally. M. Brown didn't care what I had to say. She said Cheryl was living in the U.S. illegally and she wasn't going to be allowed back in the U.S. I turned the car around and took Cheryl to my grandma's house, where she would have to stay until I figured out what to do.

Then I drove back to Detroit to go to practice. The only solution that we had to get Cheryl back to the U.S. was to get married. So that's what we did on December 15, 1993, in a little chapel in Windsor.

Some people have a shotgun wedding. We had an M. Brown–inspired wedding. We kept our original plans for a big summer wedding intact.

But we had already been married for several months when everyone showed up for our wedding in Belleville, Ontario.

You can't have a wedding without a bachelor party story. My story is about how I clobbered a guy with a lot more anger than I usually had in my NHL fights.

We were celebrating in the Post Bar in Detroit, and sure enough a fight breaks out in the front of the place that has nothing to do with me or my party. It spills back to us and I'm lifting the women over the bar to give them a shot to be safe. I'm "gently" pushing the fight back up front, but it was getting out of hand. So we decided to get out of there, and we all headed out the back door.

I'm standing outside talking to one of the guys in my party and I see one of the combatants from the fight exit the bar and coldcock Adam Gabrielle, my best friend growing up. For no apparent reason, he just sucker punched Gabrielle. Guido, as we called him, went down like a sack of potatoes.

Five seconds later I had Guido's assailant by the throat. I banged his head against a parking meter, and blood came pouring out.

I thought about hurting him more. But I made the decision that it was time for us to leave. He must have not known who I was, or he knew he was in the wrong for attacking Guido. Either way, the police were never called about the incident.

Another memory from my rookie season was scoring my first NHL goal. It took me eight games to score it, but it came on October 21, 1993, against the Winnipeg Jets. That goal was also part of my first Gordie Howe hat trick. That seems fitting.

My game-by-game history shows two fights and 18 penalty minutes in my first seven games, and then in my third career game at Joe Louis Arena I beat Bob Essensa for my first goal.

Shawn Burr went up the wall and moved the puck to Keith Primeau. That put Primeau and me on a 2-on-1 break. Primeau was coming down the left side and I was coming down the right and he sent the puck across to me at the top of the circle.

I wired a wrist shot low glove-side to beat Essensa. At that time, I was using my vintage red-and-white Louisville stick.

There was some sadness associated with that goal because my grandfather, Jigs, had died of prostate cancer the summer before my rookie NHL season. He watched me play once in the American League, and he had seen me play an NHL exhibition game the season before. But it bothered me that he never saw me play in the NHL.

He was in terrible shape when I went to see him for the last time. He was asleep, but when I held his hand he woke up and looked at me. I don't handle death very well. It makes me cry to even think about our last moments together. He was such an inspiration in my life. I wonder if I would have still found so much trouble in my life had he lived longer. He could get through to me in a way that others couldn't.

A few days after I scored my first goal, I took the first-goal puck to Woodslee, Ontario, and buried it, along with my first hockey card, in my grandfather's grave.

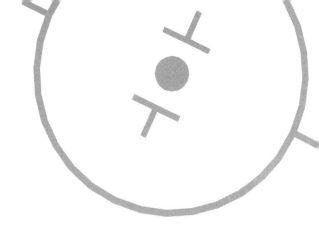

Chapter 4

The Grind Line

*"Hello out there, we're on the air,
it's 'Hockey Night' tonight"*

—"The Hockey Song"
Stompin' Tom Connors

The Grind Line

For 10 years I sat next to the grumpiest man in hockey. That's the label I hung on my Detroit Red Wings teammate Slava Kozlov.

Every day, Kozlov would walk into the dressing room and I would say, "Good morning, Koz."

"Fuck you, Mac," he would reply.

That's the NHL version of love and affection. Every retired player tells the same story: they miss the dressing room camaraderie more than they miss the on-ice competition. What I miss is being around the guys. In all the years I played, I don't think there was a single teammate that caused me any long-term anger.

When I played with the Red Wings, we were like a band of brothers.

Many times there were scrums in the corner where Kirk Maltby and Kris Draper would be tangled up with a couple of opposing players. Naturally, I moved in to help my teammates

As I was pulling guys off, an opposing player would yell at me, "How can you stick up for these guys? Maltby and Draper are assholes."

"They are assholes," I agreed, "but they're my assholes."

Even the guys I was beating on would laugh.

The NHL lifestyle breaks down to working out, playing games, and killing time between working out and playing games.

Most fans would guess that players fill the hours with drinking and carousing, and I certainly did my share of that. But do you really want to know the No. 1 leisure activity for the Red Wings on those 1997 and 1998 Stanley Cup teams?

It was solving the *USA Today* crossword puzzles. I'm not making this shit up.

I remember Stu Grimson used to do crosswords in the mid–1990s. But the crossword phase started when the Red Wings signed Joey Kocur as a free agent a couple days after Christmas in 1996. Kocur had started his career with the Red Wings in 1984–85, and had then been dealt to the New York Rangers in 1991. They dealt him to Vancouver the previous March.

Kocur was brought in for his toughness and leadership, and the leadership was evident from the moment he walked in the room. Everyone in the league knew that Kocur was close with Steve Yzerman, and no opponent wanted to see first-hand what that friendship meant to Kocur. Yzerman always got plenty of room on the ice because no one wanted to have a meeting scheduled with Kocur.

All of a sudden Kocur's interest in crosswords became the Red Wings' interest in crosswords. We called Kocur "Papa" because he was the head of our house.

He was the best I ever saw at crosswords. He could head to the toilet stall to take a dump before practice, and have the *USA Today* crossword completed when he was done doing his business.

Kocur could also complete the *New York Times* crossword puzzles during the week. He was amazing.

Kocur was also in charge of all gaming, meaning he ran all of our Super Bowl and NCAA tournament pools and all other games of chance.

When you entered these pools, you accepted the fact that you were actually competing for second place. That was because the No. 1 rule when Joey was involved with a competition was simple: Joey wins.

It didn't matter what you were playing. If Joey was playing, Joey was going to win.

One of my fondest memories of playoff hockey, by the way, involves the Chinese poker games that Mathieu Dandenault, Tim Taylor, Kocur, and I would play when we stayed in downtown hotels during the playoffs.

Leadership takes on many forms. And Joey got us all to use our brains more than we had. There were always crossword puzzles in our dressing room. Brent Gilchrist, Brendan Shanahan, Kris Draper, even the trainers were usually involved.

You would get stumped on a question and you would ask a teammate, and then suddenly you would have five players working on one crossword puzzle.

When Brett Hull joined the team in 2001, he was the king of the crossword.

Shanahan and I were roommates for a while, and crosswords fit well into our relationship. When we weren't doing that we spent a fair amount of our leisure time in some form of trivia contest, usually *Jeopardy!* or movie trivia.

We got along great, other than the fact that Shanny always did his stretching routine in the buff.

"Dude," I would say, "I don't want to see your junk."

He'd just laugh and carry on with his exercises. That's about as big of a disagreement as we ever had.

Part of our daily routine was watching *Jeopardy!* together. We kept track of our success on a piece of paper. The Red Wings have an employee named Leslie Baker who serves food to the players and their families, and she would play along after the morning skate.

I'll confess that Shanahan won more times than not because he was better at the metrosexual categories, such as literature and fashion. Sorry, but I'm just not going to know the fucking sisters names in *Little Women*. But I'm solid in the sports, history, current events, and entertainment categories.

Shanahan was a clever dude, and you are not often going to win a war of words with him. Sean Avery discovered that when he tried to trash-talk Shanahan after the Red Wings traded Avery and Maxim Kuznetsov to Los Angeles to get Mathieu Schneider.

You have to remember that Avery lived with Brett Hull when he first arrived in the NHL, meaning he studied from the master when it came to saying what was on his mind.

I liked Avery and I thought he had a good heart, but his mouth got him into too much trouble. He just never understood that Hullie could get away with saying anything just because he was Hullie. Avery didn't have the same license that Hullie had.

When we played L.A. for the first time, Avery was doing all that he could to get under Shanahan's skin. From the bench, Avery was motherfucking Shanny at every opportunity. He was giving Shanny some serious shit.

Finally, Shanny had had enough. He turned around and said, "Hey, Sean, shut the fuck up."

Shanahan was far from done. "Why are acting like this?" Shanny asked him. "Because before the game you were in our room telling us how much you hated the coach and how much you hated your teammates. What'd you call them? A bunch of fags? You've been calling me every night bitching about how bad it is in Los Angeles. So shut the fuck up."

Guys on our bench were laughing their asses off.

The dressing room can produce laughs like a comedy club. Draper liked to deliver pies to your face on your birthday. And Chris Osgood was the king of practical jokes. He liked to cut out pictures and then paste the heads of his teammates on them to create hilarious images. I think the best way to describe his work is just to say that Ozzie believes that none of us own the correct bodies for our heads. There is some of Osgood's artwork back in the Detroit weight room that still makes me laugh.

The best prank Osgood pulled on me came when I happened to doze off at the Post Bar during a night of revelry. Osgood and Draper roomed together in the Riverfront Apartments, and they brought me back to their place to sleep off the booze.

What I didn't know is that while I was sleeping, Osgood had taken out a marker and drawn all over my face. I had arching eyebrows and a Rollie Fingers moustache. I looked like a seven-year-old playing dress up.

Of course, when I woke up, it was late, and I had to hit the ground running, and I never looked in any mirror. I showed up in the dressing room with Osgood's artistry still visible on face. Osgood was the magic marker king.

Guys seemed to think it was the funniest thing they had ever seen.

Osgood had a baby face and he always looks like the model for innocence, but whenever there was a prank pulled, he was always the No. 1 suspect. The man is an evil genius in a very fun way.

On the team plane, Osgood and Maltby would always sit next to each other, giving them ample opportunity to conspire on shenanigans to keep us laughing. They were a formidable duo when it came to pranks. They were conniving SOBs.

One of my favorite Osgood jokes was one he pulled on one of his buddies from Medicine Hat, Alberta. We were all at Osgood's bachelor party weekend, and Osgood's partner in crime this time was former pro goalie Neil Little, who was one of Ozzie's buddies.

When one of their buddies had too much to drink and was sleeping it off, Ozzie and Little go to work writing on the back of his calves with a permanent marker. On one leg, they wrote, in big block letters, the words: I AM A. On the other leg they wrote: BOOZER.

It was like a scene out of *The Hangover*. We were all golfing the next day, and this shorts-clad buddy had no idea that the back of his legs were carrying a personal message.

During the course of the day, random people were calling him "Boozer" and he was totally perplexed. It was a four-hour laugh fest for the bachelor-party group because no one revealed what Osgood and Little had done.

Finally, on the 17th hole, one of the cart girls said, "Hey, Boozer, do you need another beer?"

"Why are you calling me that?"

"Because it's written on the back of your legs," she said.

After a night of partying, that moment was quite hilarious. Until that point, the dude had no idea he was a marked man.

Osgood is a talented man outside the net. To help celebrate one of his friend's birthdays, Osgood did a video in which he did a *Hockey Night in Canada*–style broadcast of his friend's beer-league game. Osgood's rendition even included Labatt's commercials.

Ozzie could get away with more because he was Ozzie. He and I probably could have pulled off the exact same devilish prank and received exact opposite reactions. If I did it, the reaction might have been, "What an asshole." But if Ozzie did the same thing he was viewed as the funniest man this side of Dane Cook.

If a prank went bad, no one ever thought it could be Ozzie. *How could it be Ozzie? Look at his innocent face.*

Ozzie and I played together for so long we even developed our own pregame ritual. People know that most athletes have superstitions, or as I like to call them, "routines." Some of these routines include the way players put on their equipment, or how they tape their sticks, or the order that they enter and exit the ice or arena. Drapes and Malts were always the first two on the ice before warm-ups and the game. Nick and I were the last two. As die-hard Red Wings fans know, my routine was always to be the last one off the ice. I felt that I needed to see all of my guys in front of me. I was always the last one at the net with the goalie prior to the opening faceoff.

I obviously did this to protect my guys, but I also did it so that I could utter my ritualistic words to Ozzie in net before each game. I can't remember if Ozzie and I started this in Adirondack or in our first year in Detroit, but people always asked me what I would say to Ozzie in that brief moment as I waited with him after everyone else tapped his pads. I would line up between the hash marks and stop in a squat-like position with my stick across my knees, Ozzie and I would be face to face and in homage to the classic Canadian movie *Strange Brew*, following the adventures of Bob and Doug McKensie, I would tap one of Ozzie's pads and say, "Keep you stick on the ice." Then I'd tap the other pad and say, "Watch your short side." Then I'd slap both pads and finish with "Stop 'em all." Then I'd skate by and tap his right post and circle or peel into the corner and the game would begin.

This happened every single game that we played together. Even after we both left Detroit and came back after six or seven years of not playing together, we picked it right back up like we hadn't missed a beat.

Maltby was old school when it came to his pranks. If you took a swig on your water bottle and the cap came off and you found yourself drenched in liquid, you were reasonably sure Maltby was involved.

If you found your stick, or any personal item, missing or in a strange place, it was usually Maltby's doing.

I would have a crossword puzzle almost completed, and then it would go missing. Maltby did some of his best work fucking up my crossword endeavors.

I would leave half-finished crosswords in my dressing room stalls. When I started working on them again later, I would get stuck when my thought-to-be-correct answers wouldn't fit. Then I would look closer and I would see someone had written the word "dickhead" into my puzzle in some random place.

"Fucking Malts," I would say, chuckling to myself.

Malts also wasn't to be trusted around my Sudoku puzzles. He would find one I had already started and then scribble in a bunch of random numbers making it look like my handwriting.

I would spend five confusing minutes trying to figure out what the fuck I had been thinking before I realized that Malts had punked me again.

Before Chris Chelios came to Detroit in 1999, I had spent a good chunk of time trying to hurt him. Chelios always seemed like he was trying to maim Steve Yzerman and Sergei Fedorov, and I was forever trying to make him pay for those sins.

The problem was that Chelios could be as funny and charming as he was ruthless. He could make you laugh at the very moment you were about to fuck him up. He has the verbal skills to talk you off the ledge when your anger boils over.

I hated Chelios when I played against him, but I certainly respected him.

What I learned when Chelios arrived in Detroit was that he is the most loyal team guy you could ever meet. He looks after everyone on the team, in particular the young guys. That's why they call him "The Godfather."

He always invites the younger players to hang out with him, and he acts like he's the concierge desk for all of the veterans. Whenever you need anything, whether it be tickets, a new car, or travel reservations, Cheli knows someone who can give you a good deal.

Chelios knows everyone in every industry. When he threw a Stanley Cup celebration party at his summer mansion on Malibu Beach in California, Tom Hanks, Sylvester Stallone, Jeremy Piven, and John Cusack were among the people who showed up.

I once introduced Chelios to Kid Rock, and now Kid Rock and Chelios are the best of friends.

On top of being a great teammate, Chelios might be the hardest-working athlete I ever met. This is a guy who rides a stationary bike in a sauna.

When Chelios showed up, he stuck me with the nickname "Diesel." It didn't quite stick like "Mac" or "D-Mac," but I kind of liked it.

Osgood was king when it came to nicknames. Any of the nicknames that we threw around in private usually came from Osgood. For example, Maltby was officially "Malts" to everyone around the rink. But to Osgood, "Malts" made him think of a milk shake, so "Malts" became "Shaker."

My favorite nickname story involves Draper being called "Nailzz."

Draper was called that only because he wanted to be called that. He always admired the hustle and drive that Lenny Dykstra showed when he played for the Philadelphia Phillies in the 1990s. Dykstra's nickname was "Nails."

One day in the dressing room, Drapes pulls me aside and asks me to start using that name around the dressing room and with the media. I always had a strong rapport with the media and he knew I would have plenty of opportunities to drop in that nickname.

"You got to run with it," Draper said.

So I did, and Drapes became "Nailzz" for a while.

We were all very serious about winning, but we had fun when we played the game. Because coach Scotty Bowman liked to change his line combinations frequently, our changes could be a clusterfuck.

It was always stressful for assistant coach Barry Smith because Scotty would tell him which players he wanted on the ice and it was Smith's job to make sure we got the right people on the ice.

Smith's job was complicated because sometimes Scotty would have players on three different lines in three different shifts.

That's why the area around our bench often looked like the streets of Tokyo at rush hour. You could have 10 guys standing up believing they were going on the ice next.

Smith had the toughest job in hockey trying to keep it straight. Knowing all of that, Steve Yzerman and I would have some fun if we had a big lead in a game.

When we were bored at the end of the bench, Steve or I would yell, "Who the fuck is up?" just to see Barry get tomato-faced and flustered.

I loved doing that.

As players, we would complain about how tough Bowman was on us. But I always felt he was fair with me. I felt as if he respected what I brought to the team. He always treated me like I was a key member of the team.

One of my favorite Bowman stories involves the Sunday afternoon he invited my then four-year-old son, Griffin, into his office to watch an NHL game on TV.

Scotty was watching a St. Louis vs. Boston game in his office and I was in the training room receiving treatment for an injury. Scotty had his door open and Griffin wandered in and started watching the game.

I could hear Griffin asking him all kinds of questions, and Scotty answered them all the way a grandfather would talk to his grandson. It reminded me of my own conversations with my late grandfather when we had watched golf together years before.

They had been talking for about 20 minutes when Smith came down the hallway after taking a shower. He was wrapped in a towel and ready to head into the coaching room.

As he was about to go in, Scotty jumped up and grabbed the door and yelled, "Fuck off, Barry, I'm finally in here talking with someone who knows the game."

Then Scotty slammed the door.

Lying on the table in the trainer's room, I had a good angle to watch Barry. His head dropped, his shoulders sagged, and he turned around and headed back to the shower area to get dressed. Scotty and Barry were the best of friends, but Scotty was probably tougher on Barry than he was on the players.

As a team, the Red Wings also had great fun at Tomas Holmstrom's expense before he became fluent in English.

Holmstrom was always one of Scotty Bowman's whipping boys. He was always in Scotty's doghouse. But Homer couldn't remember that idiom, so he would say, "I'm back in Scotty's dog yard again."

We used to tease him about being Nick Lidstrom's chauffeur because they always drove to the rink together.

If Homer got angry, he would start talking in a combination of English and Swedish. We called it Swenglish. To hear him carry on without realizing that he wasn't making sense was hilarious. Of course, we tried to make him mad as often as possible.

As soon as Holmstrom was finished with one of his Swenglish speeches, either Draper or I would turn to Lidstrom and say, "Can you translate that please?"

Goalie Kevin Hodson only played 35 games for Detroit from 1995–96 until 1998–99, but I would still say he was among my all-time favorite teammates. I think other Red Wings would say the same thing. I know Yzerman was particularly fond of him.

One of his best skills is that he could replicate the style of most of the top goalies in the league. So when we were playing Colorado in the playoffs, Hodson would play in practice in Roy's style. It was like being a scout team quarterback in football. In practice, Hodson would adjust his style to emulate the goalie we would face in the next game. It was a very helpful skill.

Hodson was diagnosed with Wolff-Parkinson-White syndrome, which results in an irregular and rapid heartbeat. He had surgery in February of 1996, and Kris Draper cut out a paper heart and drew a crack through it and taped it to Hodson's dressing stall. He wrote the word "Ticker" on it and the nickname stuck.

Ticker was an engagingly energetic and funny guy who would do anything he could to help his team. He was also a prankster, and one of his signature moves resulted in him being called "The Turd Burgler."

On the road, where dressing rooms are small and bathrooms are cramped, Ticker would purposely wait until he got to the rink to take the largest dump in the history of mankind.

He would stink up the place and then leave the pile for the next player to discover.

That's a story about Ticker that you didn't read in the *Detroit Free Press*. Bathroom humor plays well in an NHL dressing room.

One night, several of the Detroit players all went out to the Royal Oak Music Theater. We rented some limousines and got into our seats and all of a sudden Ticker comes running up to me like he had just witnessed a murder.

"There's a fight outside and they're going to kill Ozzie," he blurted out.

Up I jumped and flew out the door, where I discovered a bouncer was holding Draper, not Ozzie, upside down. Quickly I sorted out that the incident had resulted from a case of mistaken identity. The bouncers were responding to a problem and had grabbed Draper by mistake.

But my memory of that event will forever be the look on Ticker's face as he reported that one of our teammates was in trouble.

I always had great respect for the Russians on our team. Early in my career, Sergei Fedorov was extremely nice to me. One of my favorite times with Sergei was the night Cheryl and I went out with Sergei and his girlfriend to a concert at Cobo Arena that featured the Meat Puppets and Stone Temple Pilots. Sergei rented a limousine and made Cheryl and I feel like we had hit the big-time.

Sergei was a misunderstood player. He was one hell of a talented player, and when he was on his game he was as dominant as any center in the game.

Igor Larionov had the nickname of "The Professor" because he had such an intellectual aura about him. He was a true student of the game. I loved going out to dinner with him and hearing the stories about playing for Viktor Tikhonov. The stories we had about playing for tough coaches aren't even in the same league with Larionov's frightening tales of playing 11 months per year for the national team. Players from Larionov's era couldn't be sure what would happen to them if they got out of line. Being an athlete behind the Iron Curtain was a scary existence. Larionov was a great mentor for us all.

I always loved playing dominos with Larionov, Pavel Datsyuk, and Sergei Tchekmarev (our masseuse). Larionov was also the one who got me interested in English Premier League soccer. To this day, I remain a Manchester United fan because of Igor.

When Slava Fetisov joined the team in 1995, he introduced us all to a Russian card game called Helicopter. It's a trick-taking game, and if you don't take any tricks you have to match the pot.

This game became part of the flight plan for Redbird 1. There would be an "A" game, where the pots would reaches thousands of dollars, and there would be a "B" game, where the pots would be hundreds of dollars.

Games would continue once we landed. We were on a Western road trip, staying in Santa Monica, California, one night when defenseman Jamie

Pushor was playing in a hand that included a pot that was more than his bi-monthly paycheck. At the time, Pushor's yearly salary was $275,000.

That was after I'd stopped drinking, but I was chewing tobacco and I would sit at the table with a spitting cup.

Pushor was so nervous about the hand that he grabbed my spitting cup, thinking it was his beer. The tobacco hit his lips before he knew he had made a mistake.

That's when I offered to buy his hand, figuring he didn't need the pressure. I took one trick, which was enough to earn Pushor back his money.

You could walk away from the table with some pretty major losses. Mike Vernon was indebted to Fetisov for like $60,000, but it became customary for guys to forgive the debt for a lump-sum cash payment. You would give 10 or 20 percent of the debt in cash and all was good.

If you're going to gamble as teammates, it has to be a friendly game. You can't afford to have your team harmony disrupted by a gambling debt. That was not going to happen with our team. We were too close.

Draper and I were close from the beginning. We were less than 11 months apart in age, and we were both Ontario Hockey League alumni who were thrilled to have the opportunity to play in the NHL.

Our personalities are completely different, but we always had a good time together. Draper may strike you as a pretty straight-laced guy, and that's a fair assessment, but he and I did get into some minor trouble together once.

Draper wasn't a fighter on the ice, but he liked to wrestle off the ice. He was always challenging me to wrestling matches when we roomed together. The more we drank, the more interested Drapes became in testing himself against me.

He was amazingly strong in his lower body. When he worked out, he would broad jump on and off tables to help build strength in his legs. He was very difficult to knock off his feet, which is why we had some epic wrestling matches.

Our wildest wrestling match came in Boston on November 2, 1995. I know that because I remember it came after a 6–5 overtime win against the Boston Bruins. Steve Yzerman scored the game-winner.

Before the game, Bowman decided that Keith Primeau and Kris Draper would be healthy scratches. That was important because it meant that Drapes had a head start in the drinking department. By the time I showered and dressed and met them at an Irish pub, Draper was already feeling no pain. That was before my first rehab stint, so it didn't take me long to catch up.

At some point in the process, we began drinking Irish car bombs. To construct that destructive drink you add Bailey's Irish Cream and Jameson's Irish whiskey to three-quarters of a pint of Guinness stout. That drink will blow you up instantly.

Drapes and I were roommates at that point in our career. By the time we returned to our room at the Long Wharf Marriott, it was around 2:00 AM. I have no idea how the hell we ended up wrestling at that time of night, but our inebriated state probably was the primary reason that we began throwing each other around the room. It looked like a scene from a Western barroom fight. At one point, Drapes drove me into a round table and the top just snapped off the base.

As Ron Burgundy said in *Anchorman*, "Boy, that escalated quickly. I mean that really got out of hand quickly."

No one got killed with a trident, but a few pieces of furniture suffered mortal wounds.

Someone from hotel security came up three different times to tell us that our neighbors were complaining about the noise.

This was not our first wrestling match, nor was it our last. Our matches usually started out as a lighthearted competition and ended with me cracking Drapes with a quick left or a forearm shiver. This night, I caught Draper with an elbow to his face, causing his nose to bleed profusely. It hemorrhaged like a war wound.

Meanwhile, the room looked like a battlefield. If you marked it off with yellow tape it would have looked like a crime scene. Draper's blood was pooled all over.

We used the fluffy, white Marriott towels in a futile attempt to stop the bleeding quickly. The sheets and bed linens were also soaked in blood, then stacked in the bathroom. It looked like we'd performed surgery in there.

We tried to straighten the room the best we could, but it was a mess. As we left the next morning, I remember making one final effort to put the table back together. I carefully placed the top on the stand. But I wasn't fooling anyone. The minute someone touched that tabletop it was going to fall off.

About a week later we were called into the office by the Red Wings secretary, who informed us that the team had been charged $3,000 for damage to the room. I wrote a check for $1,500 on the spot and Draper had his in by the next day. Neither of us questioned the charges.

Yzerman was another guy like that. He didn't get to mix it up much on the ice, but just like Draper he liked to wrestle around with the guys in the dressing room.

One of my jobs with the Detroit Red Wings was to protect Steve Yzerman, and one night in Phoenix I failed in that duty when Yzerman almost went flying out of a 20th floor hotel window because of that roughhousing.

Yzerman always came across as Mr. Serious on television, but he was a different guy when he was hanging out with his teammates. He was the master of biting, one-line humor that would make you laugh and cringe at the same time.

When he would jab you with one of his zingers, you would say to yourself, *That's funny. I hope he was kidding.*

We were roommates early in my career, and he was trying to get the best of me in a wrestling match. It wasn't going to happen, but he's fucking Yzerman, meaning he never quit trying.

The most memorable Red Wings wrestling match happened one night in our 20th floor room at the Hyatt Hotel in Phoenix. It was two nights before we were scheduled to play the Coyotes, and Yzerman, Kris Draper, Joey Kocur, and I were in my room before heading out to dinner.

Per his tradition, Yzerman jumped on me and I pulled him off and stuffed his ass in the 18 inches of space between the bed and the wall.

Watching all of this, Kocur did what he always did—he stood up for Yzerman, and he did so by grabbing Draper and repeatedly punching him in the kidney.

Draper wants no part of a battle with Kocur, and so he's urging me to let Yzerman go.

"I'm going to be pissing blood tomorrow if you don't let Yzerman go," he yelled each time Kocur hammered on his body.

Three times I tried to pull Kocur off Draper while still keeping Yzerman stuffed between the bed and wall. Every time I would get a grip on Kocur, Yzerman would squirm and make progress toward escape. I would have to shove him back down in his hole. When I would do that, I would lose my grip on Kocur. Finally, I let Yzerman go to spare Draper further punishment.

It should be noted that my hotel room door was always open and our teammates were coming in and out as our match was going on.

Everyone was laughing pretty hard when I finally paroled Yzerman— but not before I presented him with a wickedly painful charley horse punch to this thigh. I'm sure it left a mark.

Kocur released Draper. Order seemed to be restored. I was standing by the bed, wondering where we should go to dinner. That's when Yzerman hurled himself at me, launching off the bed like he had bounced off a trampoline.

The problem was that Yzerman was far enough away that I had time to move out of the way and he went flying past me. The potential horror of that event didn't hit any of us until Yzerman's body thudded loudly against the window.

The glass held and Yzerman almost seemed to slide to the floor in slow motion like he was a cartoon character.

My guess was there were about a dozen Red Wings watching our wrestling show when Yzerman hit the window.

Can you imagine the headline? REVERED RED WINGS CAPTAIN FALLS TO DEATH BECAUSE OF HORSEPLAY.

No one in the room said a word for several seconds, all of us undoubtedly contemplating the tragedy that we narrowly averted.

"Want to get some dinner?" Kocur asked.

Sure, we said, and all filed out of the room as if nothing had happened.

For the record, Draper did piss blood the next day, just as he predicted.

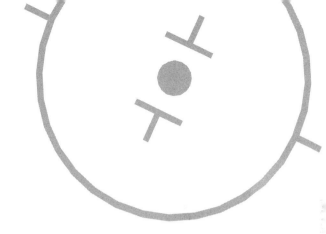

Chapter 5
Learning How to Win

"I get knocked down but I get up again,
never gonna keep me down"

—"Tubthumping"
Chumbawamba

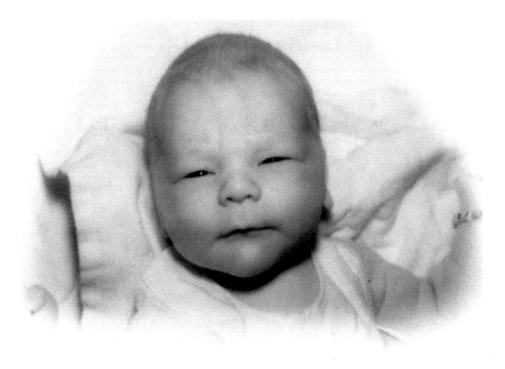

April 1, 1972—the day I was born.

Two years old and already playing hockey.

10 years old and playing my second-favorite sport.

Belleville Bulls teammates Craig Fraser, Jake Grimes, and me.

Hanging out in Belleville with my teammates.

Me and Grandpa Jigs.

Me and Coach Brian Drumm— he was my coach, mentor, and billet when I played Jr. B for the Perborough Roadrunners.

My biological father, Doug Francottie, was a cop. I never knew him growing up.

My stepdad, Craig McCarty, was the man who raised me. His death in 1999 is still hard for me to deal with to this day.

Scoring the winning goal against the Flyers in the '97 Stanley Cup Finals.
(AP Images)

*Holding the '97 Cup
with Grandpa Jigs'
wife, my grandmother
Jean (GiGi) Pritchard.*

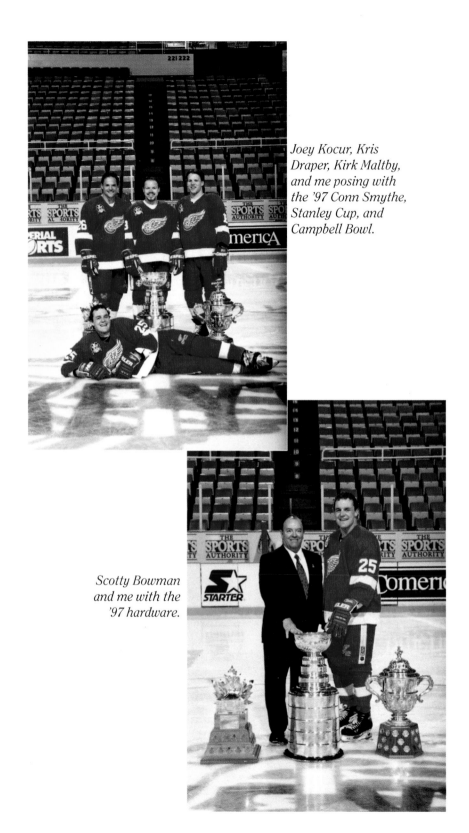

Joey Kocur, Kris Draper, Kirk Maltby, and me posing with the '97 Conn Smythe, Stanley Cup, and Campbell Bowl.

Scotty Bowman and me with the '97 hardware.

Performing with Grinder

Visiting Bill Clinton and the White House with the 1998 Stanley Cup champion Red Wings, with injured teammate Vladimir Konstantinov and team masseur Sergei Mnatsakanov.

Freddie Olausson, Mathieu Dandenault, me, Boyd Devereaux, and Kris Draper in 2002.

Boyd Devereaux and me singing with Kid Rock at the Jefferson Beach Marina after we won the Stanley Cup in 2002.

After the 2002 Cup party held at my house, I rode away in Probie's bike "Moo Moo Cow."

Learning How to Win

As the New Jersey Devils celebrated their Stanley Cup championship in 1995 on the ice at Brendan Byrne Arena, a few of us forced ourselves to watch. It was our self-imposed punishment for not getting the job done.

I specifically remember Kris Draper saying, "We are never, ever going to let this happen to us again."

Despite Draper's promise, the following season we set an NHL record of 62 wins and still didn't win the Stanley Cup. We registered 131 points that season, the highest point total produced by any team since Scotty Bowman's Montreal Canadiens had 132 points in 1976–77.

We ranked first in goals-against and first in penalty killing, and we were third overall in goal scoring. We went 13 games (12–0–1) at one point without losing, and twice we registered nine-game winning streaks. We had six 20-goal scorers, and had the third-highest scoring team in the league.

But the Colorado Avalanche, playing their first season in Denver after moving from Quebec City, took us out in the playoffs in six games.

In that the Western Conference Final, Claude Lemieux had been suspended for a game for punching Slava Kozlov. Then in Game 6, he checked Draper from behind and drove him face-first into the boards. It happened near enough to the Detroit bench that we could all hear the bones in Draper's face being crushed by the blow. It was a sickening sound.

Draper suffered a broken nose, severe facial cuts, and a fractured jaw that required surgery. His teeth and jaw had to be wired shut and he wasn't able to eat solid foods for six weeks.

For his crime, Lemieux was suspended for the first two games of the Stanley Cup Final, when the Avalanche played the Florida Panthers. In hindsight, that would turn out to be only a small part of his punishment.

There was a lot of talk in the newspapers and on talk radio about how the Red Wings needed to get bigger, stronger, and tougher. Some of my teammates said Lemieux would pay a price down the road, but honestly, Draper and I never had a real conversation about the topic. He didn't ask me to go after Lemieux. There was no master plan for exacting revenge.

When I picked Drapes up at the hospital, it wasn't as if Lemieux was a main topic of conversation.

While we were driving home, I simply said, "I'll take care of this."

That was all that was said. There was no lengthy discussion about when it would be done, or how it would be done. Draper really couldn't say much because his jaw was wired. Mostly I told him about our plans to get all of the boys together to go to the U.S. Open at Oakland Hills.

When Draper had his mouth wired up, it represented the only time during our long friendship that he has ever shut up long enough for me to say much of anything.

All of us were concerned about what Lemieux did to Draper, but we were also concerned that we had lost the series. Within the organization, there was clearly a discussion about whether we had the right mix to win a championship.

As players, we wondered that ourselves. Before the 1995 Stanley Cup Final, Detroit veteran Dino Ciccarelli had warned us not to squander our chance because you can't be sure you will ever return to the Stanley Cup Final.

"You have to take advantage of it when you get to the Final," Ciccarelli said.

When we lost to the Colorado Avalanche in 1996, many of us remembered Ciccarelli's warning and wondered whether we would ever reach the Final again.

Obviously, we did play in the Stanley Cup Final again, and we won three championships in a span of six seasons. When I look back at those glory years, it's clear to me that the key factors that resulted in us coming together as a team were the trade for Brendan Shanahan, signing Joey

Kocur out of the beer league, and our ability to exorcize our Colorado Avalanche demons.

Shanahan was acquired from the Hartford Whalers on October 9, 1996, the day of our home opener against the Edmonton Oilers. We gave up Paul Coffey and Keith Primeau, both of whom had been in Scotty's doghouse, plus a first-round pick to get Shanahan and Brian Glynn.

Shanahan dramatically changed our team in a variety of ways. He was a big, physical player who could fight and score goals. He stood up for his teammates. He was a presence on the ice and in the room.

Shanny was only a few years older than Martin Lapointe and me, but he taught us so much. I couldn't one-time the puck worth a damn until Shanny worked with me. Shanahan had one of the best one-timers in the league, right up there with Brett Hull.

I remember playing on a line with him, and asking him where he wanted the puck when I passed it to him.

"Just put it somewhere near me," he said.

That's truly all you needed to do. I could pass the puck to his front foot, his back foot, or anywhere in between, and Shanny, a right-hand shot, would open up, adjust his body, and then rocket the puck on net. Even if he didn't score, he would always end up with a great scoring chance. It was an impressive skill.

He worked with Marty Lapointe on being a goal scorer. Many times after practice, Shanny, Lapointe, and I would stay on the ice and work on our shots or talk about what goes into playing a power forward role. It was Shanny who helped me learn how to better pick my spots for fighting.

The importance of the Kocur acquisition is often overlooked. He was out of hockey, playing defense in a recreational league in summer hockey when Ken Holland signed him to give us more toughness. He was called "Papa" for a reason; he was a fatherly figure who brought a calming influence to our dressing room.

He had helped the New York Rangers win a Stanley Cup in 1994. He had done it all, and seen it all, and when the pressure started to build he had the ability to get us to relax.

On the ice he was an intimidating presence. Nobody wanted to fuck with us because they were fearful that they would have to face Joey. As I previously mentioned, he was a scary fighter.

But off the ice he was just as effective. Our captain, Steve Yzerman, considered Kocur a close friend, meaning that Kocur was in the leadership inner circle. The younger players worshipped Kocur, meaning he was considered one of the boys.

I always felt that Mike Vernon also never got enough credit for helping us develop into a championship team. He came to Detroit in 1994 in a trade for Steve Chiasson and he taught us all how to battle.

The day he showed up in Detroit, we all went out and I remember thinking, *This guy is going to be fucking awesome.*

He was funnier than hell, and it was clear that he was a team-first guy. What we soon discovered is that this little guy battled and battled and battled like his life depended on each save. Yet when the game was over he had that Western Canadian cowboy attitude of not letting anything bother him. He could let go of a game the minute it was over, and that trait is crucial for a goalie. He didn't dwell on what happened yesterday.

In addition to what he gave us in the net, Vernon was also the perfect mentor for Chris Osgood. He helped Osgood develop that hardened edge that you need to shake off bad games or bad plays. Without Vernon's tutoring, I wonder whether Ozzie would have been the same goalie he turned out to be. By the time Vernon left, Ozzie was very similar to Vernon in terms of their mental approach to playing the position.

We were all coming into our prime years at the same time. At the start of the 1996–97 season I was 24, Maltby was 24, Ozzie was almost 24, Draper was 25, Marty Lapointe and Holmstrom were 23, Nick Lidstrom and Sergei Fedorov were 26, and Shanahan was 27.

You have to lose to learn how to win. We needed to have that experience against New Jersey and getting beat by Colorado in 1996. It hardened us. It gave us a better understanding of what needed to be done.

There were multiple reasons why we didn't beat New Jersey. If you ask Scotty Bowman, he might say we lost because New Jersey defenseman Scott Niedermayer dropped his stick and my teammate Shawn Burr picked it up for him. Niedermayer then beat Burr down the ice to score on Mike Vernon. I saw the video years ago, and it wasn't exactly like that. And none of the players actually blamed Burr for the loss.

I think we lost to New Jersey because the Devils were clicking on all cylinders. Plus, we simply didn't know how to deal with the clutch-and-grab style that was more prevalent in the Eastern Conference.

More important, we didn't possess the "fear of failure" that you need to be a champion. We didn't know how to deal with being a favorite.

There was probably another event that happened before the 1996–97 season that perhaps contributed to our success. I confronted my substance abuse issues for the first time.

By then, my problem was starting to affect my work. I never played high, and I tried to time my drinking binges to make sure I was ready to play games. But all of my teammates knew what was going on because I started to become the worst practice player in NHL history. My hangovers had become a disruption to the team.

Yzerman, Paul Coffey, and Kris Draper had all had serious talks with me at various times, but I was only hearing their words, and not truly listening.

Draper tried to be my guardian angel, trying to convince me on a regular basis to "slow down" or to drink only beer and not hard liquor. I would agree to that plan, but when Drapes wasn't looking, I would sneak down to the end of the bar and line up a row of tequila or Jagermeister shots.

Then I'd look up to see Draper watching me, just shaking his head. The truth is you can't stop an alcoholic from drinking unless he or she wants to stop.

Early in my career, it seemed as if I was just like every other hockey player, going out and having a good time. But guys like Draper, Osgood, Lapointe, and others all knew when it was time to go home. They weren't continually hammered to the point that they struggled to get up in the morning.

I hung out with my teammates, but when my night was over with them, I started to find a new group of after-hour friends. I could tell Draper was concerned with the company I was keeping.

One day Scotty Bowman summoned me to his office after a particularly rugged practice and told me it was time for me to get my act together. I had embarrassed myself at practice that morning. At one point, we were skating in line rushes and Lapointe and Draper were at the net putting a shot on goal while I was still laboring to get across the blue line.

Bowman told me that he liked me as a player and that I was important, but I wasn't bigger than the team. He said I was hurting the team. Basically, he told me I had to get my shit together.

If you think that having a coaching legend dressing me down for my lifestyle would be enough to pursue sobriety, you would be wrong.

I knew when I was 20 that I had a drinking problem. My grandfather, Jigs, was an alcoholic, and I knew the signs of problem drinking. I knew I had the symptoms. When I received the news that my grandfather died in 1993, I had been at a charity event in Belleville, Ontario. I started drinking that day and didn't stop.

Angry over the loss of my grandfather, I stole a boat that belonged to the neighbor of the Bulls' owner, Dr. Robert Vaughan. I took it across the lake to attend the party. Everyone at the party knew whose boat it was. I should have been arrested. But I wasn't.

The summers of 1994, 1995, and 1996 are a blur to me because I spent the off-season drinking. I had different pods of friends and bounced from one pod to the next, mostly because I didn't want anyone to have the complete picture of how much drinking I was doing.

I would be with my friends on the east side for one night and then my friends from the west side. In many of my pods, I was put on a pedestal because I was a Detroit Red Wings player. In those pods, no one ever questioned any of my choices. The only people who were scrutinizing my behavior were teammates and family members. I began to see them less and less.

And when I was with family or teammates I always painted a rosy picture. I had been drinking since I was 15, and I had learned what to say to people to get them off my back. I could say the right thing, I just couldn't do the right things. I would lie to those trying to help me, and lie to myself about my ability to quit.

But the lying ended in the summer of 1996. I left my house one day to attend the U.S. Open at Oakland Hills. I didn't come home for a week.

Drapes and several of our friends were with me at Oakland Hills. We sat under a tree at the 18th with a tray of beers and enjoyed the tournament. Steve Jones won by one stroke over Tom Lehman and Davis Love III, but honestly I'm hazy about the details of that tournament, even though I was there every day.

At that point, I was more of a binge drinker than an everyday drinker. When I found a space in my life to drink, I took it over the edge. Normal folks go out, drink some beers, and have some fun—maybe even have a blowout night—and then they resume their normal routine. But my blowout nights would last for three or four days or longer. Once I climbed on the train, it was hard for me to get off.

Draper was the teammate who best understood that my life was starting to unravel. Even though I told Bowman that I would get my drinking under control, I had not made any lasting changes.

Sensing that I needed immediate help, Draper kept calling from his summer residence in Toronto and Cheryl had to tell him that she had no idea where I was.

At the time, I didn't know where I was either. I was drinking, partying, and crashing at whatever location I happened to be at when the room stopped spinning.

Cheryl packed up my newborn son, Griffin, and headed back to Belleville to live with her parents. When I finally emerged from my stupor, I offered her my usual babble about how I would change and get my drinking under control.

But Cheryl had heard it all before. This time, she pulled no punches, telling me bluntly I needed to get clean for the sake of my family. Griffin had been born a week before we were knocked out by the Avalanche. I'd gone on a bender when my son was only about a month old.

"I love you to death, and I always will, but I'm not going to let you do this to us," Cheryl told me. "Doing this to me is one thing. I can handle it because I know what you're like. But you are not going to do this to Griffin."

I had grown up not knowing my real father, and I had always vowed that I would be there for my kids. I've always been someone who does what he says he's going to do.

I asked myself a question that day: What's more important, booze or your family?

The answer was easy, but the solution was not. It was the middle of the summer, and I had to tell the Red Wings I was entering the Maplegrove Center for chemical dependency outpatient program in West Bloomfield, Michigan. I was concerned about what the team might do because the Red Wings had grown weary of dealing with Bob Probert's substance abuse issues.

But I remember GM Jim Devellano told me that I had taken the first step toward solving the problem by admitting it.

To be honest, I can thank Probie for the fact that my substance abuse issue didn't cause me even greater damage.

As I've said many times, I was primarily a good drunk. I never was arrested during my career, and never found myself in any serious trouble. I had witnessed what happened to Bob because of his substance abuse and I knew I did not want it to happen to me. Because of Bob's experiences, I understood the consequences of the disease.

I didn't want to follow Bob's game plan for life. I never wanted to let myself become so out-of-control that I couldn't find my way back. Because I'd witnessed what Bob went through, I knew it was time for me to seek help.

This period of time was trying for my family because my attempts to get sober came six months after my stepfather Craig had been diagnosed with multiple myeloma, a rare form of cancer. Life expectancy for people with that disease is two to three years. By that time in my life, I had started to view Craig as one of my true supporters. It was devastating news to hear that another male figure in my life was sick.

But the truth is that we bonded over our illnesses. I think we drew strength from each other. We began to mend the fences and tear down the walls that separated us. We decided to fight our battles together. Our relationship strengthened during that time period.

When I showed up at training camp that fall, my mind and body were clean and clear for the first time in years. I was focused on the mission of winning a championship.

The one thing I noticed when I was sober was that life slowed down. When I was drinking, my life was always a blur. The days blended together, particularly the days when I had been drinking to excess. It always seemed as if my brain was partly cloudy.

It seemed like there was more time to enjoy my life when I wasn't getting high or scheming to get high. It is amazing how draining it can be to be involved in a non-stop party life.

In 1996–97, when I wasn't drinking or doing drugs, I enjoyed my best NHL season, scoring 19 goals and 30 assists for 49 points.

There was certainly evidence to prove to me that being a clean-and-sober McCarty was in my best interest. But that didn't mean my battle against substance abuse would be an easy fight. Probably at that time in my life I felt like I had licked my problem. But I would soon discover that my fight was far from over.

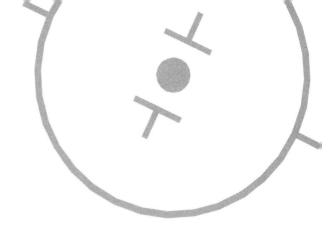

Chapter 6
Crime and Punishment

"Eye for an eye, tooth for a tooth, blood for blood"

— "Bad Company"
Five Finger Death Punch

Crime and Punishment

If you want to appreciate how much anger I was carrying when I went after Claude Lemieux on March 26, 1997, take a close look at my left fist in the famous photo where Lemieux appears to be "turtling."

My fist is so tightly wound that there is a stress indentation that runs down from hand to my forearm.

Many times since then I've tried to ball my fist tight enough to reproduce that stress line. I've never been able to do it.

Even though I fought close to 200 times during my professional hockey career, it's fair to say that I brought more intensity and anger to the Lemieux confrontation than any bout I ever had.

Years later, Lemieux told me that the first blow I delivered was the hardest punch he ever received. During my career, there were other times when I wanted to pound the shit out of an opponent, but I'd never wanted to hurt anyone as much as I wanted to hurt Lemieux.

My NHL career included 758 regular season games played, but this was the contest that defined my career. Although I have a Stanley Cup–clinching goal, this game is probably the most memorable game I ever played. It's the game that fans ask me about the most.

Some fans don't even remember that I also scored 39 seconds into overtime to give us a 6–5 come-from-behind win over the Avalanche. They just recall that I avenged Kris Draper's broken jaw and other injuries by taking down Lemieux.

The "Bloody Wednesday" game, as it has been called, was certainly the wildest game I was ever involved in. When the buzzer sounded to end that contest, the two teams had combined for 18 fighting majors.

My memorable first-period encounter with Lemieux almost didn't happen because Colorado defenseman Adam Foote grabbed me just as all hell was starting to break loose. He was strong as an old bear, and he had a tight grip on me. But Brendan Shanahan came over and gave Foote a double-arm chop.

That broke me free from Foote. It was like letting a dog off the leash.

I took a direct path toward Lemieux. It was written, and said, that Lemieux never saw me coming. But that's untrue. I can tell you that I looked him directly in the eyes before I hit him. I wanted him to know my anger. I didn't sucker punch him, as some have written. I coldcocked him.

When he went down, he ended up in what hockey players call the "turtle" position. He was covering his head with his arms. Again, much later, he told me that he wasn't turtling. He had momentarily been knocked out by the punch, and was trying to regain his senses.

Meanwhile, I was trying to hurt him. I was throwing punches and trying to slam his head into the ice. I dragged him over to the boards so Kris Draper could have a good look.

Undoubtedly, that moment was what Detroit fans had been anticipating. In the *Detroit News* that morning, a sports column had been published bearing the headline A Time for Revenge.

Accompanying the article was a photo of Lemieux made to resemble a wanted poster. It gave information about Lemieux's alleged crimes, such as "likes to attack from behind."

NHL executive Jim Gregory and security director Dennis Cunningham both attended the game with the hope of discouraging any potential trouble.

Everyone seemed to be sure that March 26 was going to be the night that I was going to try to settle the score. The funny part of that story is that I didn't truly know that was going to be the night.

I was positive that at some point I was going to exact revenge on Lemieux because of what he did to Draper. But I planned on picking my spot to accomplish that objective. Shanahan had taught me that being a good teammate also meant knowing the right time to settle a score.

You don't want to put your team in a bad position because of a personal grudge.

Draper would testify to the truth that he and I only had one conversation about me going after Lemieux and that came when I picked him up from the hospital.

This was not the first time we had played the Colorado Avalanche in Detroit after the Draper injury. We'd already played them three times that season, and we had lost all three games. But Lemieux was injured for the first two games, and I didn't want it to happen in Denver. If I was going to make Lemieux pay for his attack on Draper, it was going to be for our fans to see live.

When this book was being written, my former teammate Aaron Ward was interviewed and pointed out that he had driven to the game with Draper and me and that there had been no discussion about the game turning into a brawl.

In fact, Ward said that he had wished that I had warned him of my intentions because he would have liked to have better prepared for the gladiator-like combat that ensued that night. I didn't warn Ward because I didn't know for sure that would be the night. We needed to win that game and I felt like I shouldn't do anything to jeopardize our chances to win.

But as the game progressed, it evolved into the right time to make Lemieux pay the price for his indiscretion.

If Lemieux wants to be angry at anyone for what happened that night, he should be mad at Forsberg, because it might not have started had he not decided to tangle up with Larionov. As soon as that skirmish broke out, I was looking for Lemieux.

This game wasn't just about me settling up with Lemieux. It was about the Red Wings making the Avalanche understand that we were ready to do whatever it took to run them over en route to a championship.

This was the game where we realized who we were, and what we were about.

Bloody Wednesday was the event that brought us together as a team. Maybe some look at the game and see mayhem. What I see is the Red

Wings standing up for each other. There is nothing that builds team unity more than fighting shoulder-to-shoulder.

The fight card started with Jamie Pushor scrapping with Colorado defenseman Brent Severyn at 4:45 of the first period, and then my linemate Kirk Maltby took on Rene Corbet at 10:14.

The funny thing about the main event brawl is that it was triggered by a minor skirmish between Colorado's Peter Forsberg and Detroit's Igor Larionov. These were two unlikely combatants. You certainly wouldn't expect that gentlemanly Igor would light the match that caused the game to explode.

Forberg and Larionov collided along the boards with 1:38 left in the first period, and then started wrestling. The bell sounded in my head. After Shanahan helped me break free from Foote, a linesman grabbed me by the jersey. But I pulled free, and homed in on Lemieux. Once I had dragged him over to the boards, I also drove my knee into his head. The anger I had for him was real.

While my Lemieux ass-whipping was in progress, I had no idea that Mike Vernon and Brendan Shanahan were in the midst of their own battles.

When Shanahan saw Patrick Roy roaring from his net to defend Lemieux, he intercepted him with a full-speed collision in the middle of the ice. That prompted Foote to come to Roy's aid, and then Vernon abandoned his net to help Shanahan. Then Vernon fought Roy while Shanahan fought Foote.

Roy ended up cut. Forsberg aggravated a previous injury and didn't return to the game. Pools of blood were visible on the ice and there was a bloodstain on the boards.

Already infuriated by the beating I put on Lemieux, the Avalanche became even more enraged that I was only assessed a double-minor for roughing. They thought I should have received a gross misconduct.

Was referee Paul Devorski influenced by Lemieux's turtling? I don't know, but it really wasn't a fight in the truest sense of the word. Lemieux didn't deserve a penalty because he didn't fight back.

The Vernon vs. Roy battle, which established Vernon as a legend in Detroit, wasn't the last fight of the game. The entertainment was only beginning. Adam Deadmarsh and Vladimir Konstantinov fought shortly after. Shanahan and Foote had a rematch four seconds into the second period. Later, Mike Keane took on Tomas Holmstrom, and then Ward fought Severyn. I fought Deadmarsh and then Pushor had his second fight of the game, taking on Uwe Krupp.

People ask me whether Lemieux said anything to me during that beating, and the answer is no. He didn't have time to say anything.

The following November, we faced each other for the first time after I administered my beatdown.

He earned my respect that day by coming out and lining up right across from me on the opening faceoff. I called him every motherfucking name in the book trying to goad him into another brawl. I talked shit about his wife and kids. There was no reaction.

"Everyone hates you, you piece of shit. What are you doing out here across from me?" I said to him. "You come over here, but you aren't going to do anything?"

Kris Draper won the draw and got the puck to Nick Lidstrom, and the next thing I know Lemieux blasted me right in the nose.

I remember thinking, *Good, he's going to fight this time.*

He's bigger and stronger than I am. But my assessment was that I won the fight, although he stung me with that first blow. That seemed to be the end of our need to fight each other.

In 2002–03, Lemieux was playing for the Dallas Stars and he skated up to me like he may be looking to start something

"What the fuck do you want?" I asked. "You looking to go again?"

"No, I just want to say I'm happy for you that you're doing better in your life," he said.

He obviously had heard that I was trying to clean up my act regarding my substance abuse. To be honest, that moment changed how I viewed Lemieux.

The two of us never spoke together about the incident until 2010, when we were both guests on Michael Landsberg's *Off The Record*.

When you watch that interview, it's difficult to believe that it's the same guy who was public enemy No. 1 in Detroit. After the hit he laid on Draper, a guard had to be posted outside his hotel room to assure his security.

Lemieux said he appreciated the role that I played on the Red Wings. Landsberg asked me whether I would want Lemieux as my teammate and I said, "No."

On April 4, 2011, we met again, at the Gibraltar Trade Center for an autograph session. We were both offered $10,000 to come in and sign photos.

We talked, not about hockey, but our children. We both have sons, roughly the same age, who are playing hockey. As we talked, I could see why Shanahan and Lemieux were good friends when they played together in New Jersey. Obviously there was an off-ice Lemieux and an on-ice Lemieux. I didn't respect the on-ice Lemieux. But I did like the off-ice Lemieux.

In the *Windsor Star*, the day after our appearance at the Gibraltar Trade Center, Lemieux was quoted as saying that getting together with me was easy.

"I always actually admired the way he played, admired the way he stuck up for his teammates," Lemieux said. "I admired everything he brought to the game. But if we got on the ice today and competed, it wouldn't change the way I would play and it wouldn't change the way he played."

We were supposed to sign from 2:00 to 4:00 PM, but the crowds were so big we signed until about 8:00 that night.

Just to show how time heals all wounds, Lemieux agreed to sign "Turtle" on some of the photos he signed. He seemed to have fun at the event.

Time didn't heal everything for some fans. A few yelled "Turtle" as Lemieux walked to the signing area. Honestly, there were some who wanted me to beat up Lemieux again right there in Taylor, Michigan.

Lemieux donated his fee directly to charity. All of his signing fees go to charity.

In hindsight, I should respect Lemieux. He made no excuses for the way he played.

He played on the edge. I should understand that because I played on the edge. But I think I knew the location of the line that shouldn't be crossed. He didn't seem to know where that line was.

What is sometimes lost in the memory of Bloody Wednesday is that we won the game. To me, that was the most important aspect of what occurred on the ice. If we had won the battle, and then lost the game, it would not have had the same impact on our team. We needed to prove to ourselves that we could physically dominate them and also beat them on the scoreboard.

This was the night that the Red Wings laid the foundation for the back-to-back championships in 1997 and 1998 and another title in 2002. It was the night we started to see ourselves as an unstoppable force.

From 1996 until 2002, the Colorado vs. Detroit rivalry was the greatest rivalry in all of sports.

When you consider the storyline, the drama, the physical play, and the offensive play, that contest might have been the most entertaining game of the 1990s. The game featured 11 goals and 39 penalties, including 18 fighting majors. The Avalanche led 5–3 early in the third period, but Marty Lapointe and Shanahan scored 36 seconds apart to tie the score.

Now that I'm in retirement and living in Florida, I meet people who don't know hockey. I like to introduce them to the sport by showing them the video of that game.

At least once per year, I feel the need to pull out the tape and watch it.

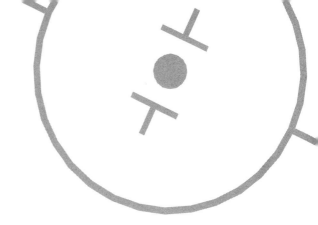

Chapter 7
Tomas Storm Trooper

*"You can do this if you try, all I want
for you my son, is to be satisfied"*

—"Simple Man"
Lynyrd Skynyrd

Tomas Storm Trooper

Only once in my NHL career was I able to beat a defenseman one-on-one. But it came at the best possible moment. Timing is everything in life.

I used an inside-out move to beat Philadelphia's Janne Niinimaa, and then made a sweet move around goalie Ron Hextall to score what turned out to be the Stanley Cup–clinching goal in the 1997 Final.

"What the fuck was that?" captain Steve Yzerman screamed at me as we celebrated near the boards.

"I don't know," I screamed, "but who gives a fuck!"

Yzerman's eyes were as big as dinner plates, like he had just witnessed a miraculous transformation. My scarred and battered hands had suddenly performed magic.

The play had started in our end with Vladimir Konstantionov moving the puck ahead to Tomas Sandstrom, who in turn head-manned the puck to me as I cut through the neutral zone. The Flyers were in the midst of a line shift.

Guys on the bench were yelling for me to dump the puck in, and that's what I was going to do. But as I got near the Philadelphia zone, it was like my automatic pilot engaged.

The two previous summers I had traveled to Sweden to work with stick-handling coach Tomas Storm. We worked on moving our hands back and forth, with the idea that controlling the puck would become second nature. I'd spend 10 days on the ice with him, mostly working alongside 12-, 13-, and 14-year-old players. It's no wonder that Swedish players have such exceptional hands because they spend hours upon hours learning to handle the puck.

The best player in our sessions was a 16-year-old named Kristian Huselius. I nicknamed him "Magic" because of the tricks he could do with the puck.

As I crossed the blue line in the Stanley Cup Final, I could sense Niinimaa was diving into me. I thought to myself, *Holy shit, I've got him beat.*

At that point, it was all muscle memory. Storm taught us to abandon our traditional thinking of moving the puck laterally with our stick and think about moving it north to south. If you watch Pavel Datsyuk, that's how he moves the puck.

Niinimaa moved in to knock away the puck, and I moved the puck outside and past him. Out of the corner of my eye, I could see Flyers goalie Ron Hextall driving out of the net, embracing his own plan to poke the puck off of my stick. But just like Storm had taught me, I pulled the puck back and went around him.

Suddenly, I was in the blue paint with the puck on my stick and a vacant net in front of me. My only thought was not to miss the fucking net with my shot. I guided the puck in to give us a 2–0 lead in the second period. With the way we were playing defensively, it seemed as if my goal was going to seal the deal.

The Flyers didn't score until Lindros found the net with 15 seconds left, and that made my goal the series-clinching goal that ended the 42-year NHL championship drought in Detroit.

With seven seconds left, there was a neutral-zone faceoff and I was on the ice with Yzerman, Brendan Shanahan, Konstantinov, and Nicklas Lidstrom.

Yzerman won the draw, delivering the puck to Konstantinov with the perfect touch to prevent icing. But I'm superstitious, and I don't like taking chances. Even with victory assured, I raced down the ice as if the game hung in the balance. I chased that puck with every ounce of energy I had at my disposal.

When the horn sounded, I was deep in the Philadelphia zone. As I turned around, I had a panoramic view of the ice as the boys streamed off the Detroit bench to celebrate our first Stanley Cup in 42 years. The sight of my teammates mobbing goalie Mike Vernon is a memory I will never forget.

The noise was deafening, and yet it seemed as if there was no sound as I skated toward the pile. It was like everyone was moving in slow motion.

The first person I came upon was Marty Lapointe, who had his arms stretched out to greet me with a bear hug. I jumped into his arms and we collapsed into a pile of guys. As wipeouts go, this was the greatest of my career.

What made the moment even more special was the fact that my grandmother and my stepfather were in the stands to see it. Tomas Storm was also at the game, no doubt analyzing what I had done with my hands on that play.

It was my moment. I scored the most beautiful goal of my career. I had played a big role in helping us win the Cup.

In the championship video from that season, you see me talking to referee Bill McCreary before a faceoff as more than 20,000 stand and cheer during the closing moments of the game. We called McCreary "No Bullshit Bill" because he was a straight shooter and an exceptional referee.

He looked at me, and said, "It doesn't get any better than this, does it?"

"If it ever gets better than this, you call me, okay?" I said, laughing.

Coming into the series, we had been the underdogs. The media didn't believe we could handle the Legion of Doom line. John LeClair had been a 50-goal scorer that season, and Eric Lindros had 32 goals in just 52 games. Mikael Renberg had netted 22 goals and added 37 assists for 59 points. Renberg was the small guy on the line, and he was 6'3", 226 pounds.

Five seconds into that series I hit Philadelphia defenseman Petr Svoboda so hard that he is probably still sore today. I almost put him through the glass.

I wanted that championship badly enough that I was willing to hurt a friend to get it. Paul Coffey had been my buddy in Detroit, but I steamrolled him in Game 2 and knocked him out of the series. He didn't speak to me for five years.

When we won both games in Philadelphia, I think we started to realize that we were an even better team than we thought we were.

It's fascinating to me that I ended up with the series-clinching goal because I was not a guy who needed the limelight to feel validated. I was content to be a spoke in the wheel. As long as I felt like my teammates and coaches thought I was contributing, I was a happy guy. And there was never a moment when the Red Wings made me feel anything but needed.

When the champagne was being sprayed around the dressing room, Yzerman came up to me and said that I was the lucky one because I was the only player who was clearly going to remember how we celebrated.

I wondered how I was going to react as I saw all of my teammates celebrating with booze. Draper was quoted in the newspaper as saying no player would have thought less of me had I drank champagne out of the Stanley Cup.

But I didn't do that. I didn't need to do that. I was drunk on the success of my team.

Draper and I enjoyed victory cigars that night, and when the boys took the Stanley Cup to Big Daddy's for late-night celebrations, they made sure that I didn't feel left out of the celebratory drinking from the Cup.

When they were finished drinking their fill of beer out of the Cup, one of the players fetched a towel and cleaned out Lord Stanley's mug obsessively before it was re-filled it with Coca-Cola for me.

It was a memorable night, even without drinking booze out of the Stanley Cup.

The celebration. The parade. It seemed as if we partied for a couple of days. I remember Red Wings owner Mike Ilitch came up to me at a party at his home and said, "You're my Rocky."

He always called me "Rocky" after that, and constantly told me that he thought of me as one of his sons.

Mike and Marian Ilitch treated all of their players with great respect, but I always felt as if our relationship was special. Obviously, they had a special place in their hearts for Steve Yzerman, but it seemed like they had a different place in their heart for me. They always made me feel special.

The 1997 championship revelry didn't stop until June 13, when my teammates, Slava Fetisov and Vladimir Konstantinov, along with team masseuse Sergei Mnatsakanov, were badly injured in a limousine accident on Woodward Avenue in Birmingham, Michigan, after a team party.

What haunts most of the Detroit players still to this day is that those injuries occurred despite the fact that the players and the team took precaution to assure that we wouldn't have an accident like that.

Limousines were purposely brought in to take players home because we knew there was going to be drinking at the party.

We were stunned when we were told the news. Since I had not been drinking, I drove some of the guys to the crash site. The driver of the limousine, Richard Gnida, who was driving on a suspended license, had struck a tree in the median. When we saw the wreckage of the limousine we thought it was possible that we might have fatalities. The limousine was so twisted up, I remember thinking, *No one could survive that.*

Our only thought at that point was to get to the hospital as quick as we could.

Once we arrived at the hospital, we discovered that Slava Fetisov had walked away with very minor injuries, but Vladdie and Mnatsakanov suffered serious head injuries. Both men were in comas for a long time.

As you know, Konstantinov never played again. He suffered brain damage. He can't communicate the way he once did, but I know the Vladdie we know is still inside. He certainly recognizes his teammates.

Certainly it was a tragic end to what would have undoubtedly been a great career, maybe even a Hall of Fame career. He was a warrior. I remember he and Jeremy Roenick used to battle like gladiators. One night, Roenick hit Konstantinov with such force that it shattered a pane of glass. The workers repaired it and on the next shift Konstantov hit Roenick in the same spot along the boards and the replacement panel shattered.

He might have been able to compete with Nick Lidstrom for a Norris Trophy. I never saw a defenseman better at scoring on a breakaway than Konstantinov.

The next year, the Red Wings rallied around the idea that we had to win to honor Konstantinov. We did that, finishing off the job with a sweep against the Washington Capitals. I had one of my best seasons in 1998–99. I had 14 goals and 40 points in 69 games.

That was also the first season I made $1 million. Over the next five years, my salaries would rise to $1.6 million and then to a high of $2.2 million.

You want to believe that you won't be changed by money, but money does change you. It changes the people you meet. It changes the people who want to meet you. When money is no object, you live in a world with greater temptation.

I know now that it wasn't a good situation for a person with an addictive personality. But I didn't know that then.

Another event that contributed to my downward spiral was the death of my stepdad, Craig, in 1999.

Cancer took him from his family on November 22 that year. I was supposed to be on a road trip, but I ended up with a sports hernia. Because of that, I was able to see him often, almost every day, in the days leading up to his death. I believe that things happen for a reason.

We talked about all of the issues we had when I was a kid. He explained why he did and said the things he did.

I apologized for some of the things I did and said. We cleared the air. We made peace with our relationship, and I believe he knew then how much I admired and appreciated what he did for me. Now, as I'm more in tune with my efforts to be a father, I draw on my memories of how Craig filled that role.

Near the end of his life, we had resolved all of our issues, and we shared a laugh when I said, "Now that we have all of that resolved, what do we talk about now?"

Although I knew his death was coming, I didn't handle it well, maybe because I knew in my heart and soul that losing Craig would have severe consequences. Not long after Craig's death, I started using drugs, particularly ecstasy. My marijuana use also escalated.

Today, I realize that Craig was the only person in my life who was holding me accountable at that time. I would listen to him more than anyone else. Maybe I was always trying to win his approval. My grandfather and Craig were the two male role models that mattered to me and they were both gone.

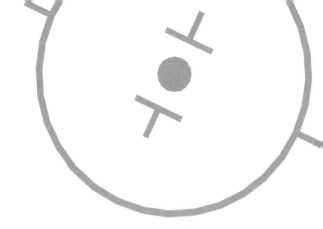

Chapter 8

2002

*"Ain't no party like a Detroit Party
cuz a Detroit party don't stop"*

—Kid Rock

2002

After I posted a hat trick against Colorado Avalanche goalie Patrick Roy in Game 1 of the 2002 Western Conference Finals, I jokingly told the media they might have just witnessed one of the seven signs of the Apocalypse.

"Get out your bibles because the end of the world must be coming," I said after our 5–3 victory.

It was the only time in my career I scored three goals in a game, and it had come against one of the greatest goalies in NHL history.

Our captain Steve Yzerman told reporters, "I have a better chance of winning the lottery than Mac has of getting a hat trick."

Counting the regular season and playoffs, I had played 650 NHL games before I finally netted my first hat trick.

Maybe I was simply due because I had only scored five goals in 62 games during the regular season and I hadn't scored a single goal in the first two rounds of the playoffs. I was never a 20-goal scorer at the NHL level, but I was good for 12 to 15 in my prime years in Detroit.

But the truth is that I always felt like I had Roy's number during my NHL career. When you're a pro hockey player, there are always goalies you feel like you can't beat. These guys always find a way to get a glove, or a stick, or an arm on your shots. They get in your head. You just expect them to stop your shot.

Then there are goalies that seem to be vulnerable to whatever offensive magic you happen to have on any given night. I always believed I could blast my shot past Roy. I don't know why. I just did.

Plus, although I did not boast a staggering number of goals in my career, I did own several important goals. I always felt that I would show up center stage when the spotlight shone brightest.

Clearly, the Colorado vs. Detroit series qualified as a major event. Many media members wrote that this series was the true Stanley Cup Final. The media expected the winner of this series to coast to the NHL championship. That's not how we viewed it, but it is what the pundits were saying. The Avalanche were the defending Stanley Cup champion, and we were only four years removed from winning back-to-back titles.

USA Today offered that our series featured more Hall of Fame players than any NHL playoff series since the New York Islanders and Edmonton Oilers played in 1984.

What made the hat trick sweeter was the fact that Colorado coach Bob Hartley had decided to play Joe Sakic and Peter Forsberg together and the Grind Line was on the ice against them quite a bit. It was clear that we won that exchange.

In the newspaper the next day, Detroit coach Scotty Bowman was quoted as saying, "It was a wonderful effort from a guy who gives his all every game. They were all great goals. There wasn't anything lucky about any of them."

The score was tied 2–2 going into the third period of that game. At 1:18 of the period, I put us ahead by firing a laser shot past Roy from the high slot. I used Colorado defenseman Adam Foote as a screen.

Just after the halfway mark of the period, I ended up on a 2-on-1 break with Kirk Maltby.

A 2-on-1 seemed to be a regular occurrence for Maltby and me, and we enjoyed bickering about what should happen when I had the puck in those situations.

"You always look me off—it's like I'm not even there," Maltby would complain.

"Yeah," I would say, "but you're the best decoy duck in the league."

Sure enough, in this game, I used Maltby as a decoy and then went high on the glove-side to beat Roy at 12:44. With Roy in the net, I never thought pass.

My third goal came at 15:15 when I found a rebound and tucked it quickly under the crossbar.

That game was played on May 18, and I know that because my son Griffin's birthday was on May 20. He turned six that year. The reason I remember that clearly is that I had asked Griffin the day before the series opened what he wanted for his birthday.

"Dad," he said, "I want you to score a goal tomorrow."

"I'll do my best," I said.

When Game 1 was over, Griffin was in the runway to greet me as I came off the ice.

"I know you wanted one goal, but I got three. Hope that's okay," I said.

He gave me the biggest hug I ever received from him. There is no greater feeling than making one of your children happy.

Perhaps this will surprise you, but I had the utmost respect for Roy. I always admired his passion and fiery personality. I liked the way he stood up for his team. I appreciated his gladiator mentality.

The Avalanche had won the Stanley Cup the season before, and we didn't expect them to fold up after losing Game 1. We were correct in that assessment. As we had anticipated, the series was angry, physical, and tight. Three of the first five games went to overtime and we were down 3–2 in the best-of-seven series going into Game 6 in Denver.

It seemed as if all the breaks had gone against us in that series, but we got a big one in Game 6 when Patrick Roy dropped the puck after making a big save against Yzerman. Shanahan was there to poke the puck over the goal line to give us a 1–0 lead.

In the second period, I had a 2-on-1 shorthanded break with Malts and of course I was thinking shot all of the way. I looked far side against Roy, and saw nothing. So I blasted it short-side and it zipped past Roy.

"When I'm on a 2-on-1 with DMac I just look for the rebound," Maltby said.

What I remember most about Game 7 was getting a 4–0 first-period lead and feeling as if it was the scariest four-goal lead an NHL team had ever owned.

During the intermission between the first and second periods, you could have heard a pin drop in our dressing room. It was as quiet as a library, and that was unusual. There was always chatter in our room between periods.

We were a confident team, but we were shocked to be ahead 4–0 in that game. Tomas Holmstrom had scored on our first shot, 1:57 into the game, and then Fedorov put us ahead 2–0 80 seconds later. Robitaille added a goal midway through the period, and then Homer added his second off a Robitaille rebound. We had four goals on 10 shots against a goalie who had already won two Game 7s in that postseason.

At that point, Roy had played 240 playoff games and had never before given up four goals in the first period of a postseason game. Hockey players are generally superstitious, and no one wanted to jinx our lead by talking about it.

It was like being in a baseball dugout when a pitcher has a perfect game going and no one is saying a word about it.

Honestly, that four-goal lead was probably one of the most stressful situations of my life. The Detroit roster in 2001–02 included Yzerman, Hasek, Robitaille, Nick Lidstrom, Chris Chelios, Sergei Fedorov, Brett Hull, Igor Larionov, and Brendan Shanahan. We were a Hall of Fame team. We had nine guys on that team who were 35 and older and 17 guys who were 30 or older. We were supposed to win it all.

Sometimes, the fear of losing can be a catalyst for success. We weren't mentally prepared to have a big lead. It was like we didn't know how to act. Suddenly, the four-goal lead seemed like the worst lead in hockey. In our minds, we started worrying about the Avalanche chipping away at our lead. They certainly had the explosiveness to score five goals over the final 40 minutes.

Our objective for the second period was not to give up an early goal that would allow the Avalanche to regain some momentum.

We really didn't start to breathe easy until Hull scored less than five minutes into the second. Then Fredrik Olausson scored and Roy was pulled from the game. The final score was 7–0.

Yzerman said after the game, "We thought it would be a 1–0 game, or go into overtime, or be a 2–0 game. We were thinking after the first period—*This isn't the way it's supposed to be.*"

Hasek posted back-to-back shutouts in Game 6 and Game 7. Dom had his quirkiness, but you won't find a goalie who competed any harder than he did.

It was not out of the ordinary for him to spend the night in the dressing room if he wasn't happy with the way he played in a game. He didn't want to take his anger home. I was always one of the first players to practice, always showing up about two hours before start time. Dom would always be there, sometimes curled up on the couch with a towel draped over him as a blanket.

The Detroit vs. Colorado rivalry was as intense as it gets, and the animosity was real. We hated those fuckers and they hated us. But the truth is that we brought out the best in each other.

I respected how the Avalanche played. Foote was such a ruthless competitor that he forced me to be a better player. When I was sitting on the bench, I found myself always watching how Joe Sakic played.

I thought Forsberg was a great player. He was the first player I ever saw use the reverse shoulder check that current Red Wings player Pavel Datsyuk is famous for today. Forsberg hit harder when he had the puck than when he didn't. If you tried to hit him when he possessed the puck, he would lower his shoulder and drive it into you. It felt like you were being hit by a bag of cement.

One memory I have of Forsberg is a slashing episode we had during a faceoff in a playoff game. We were at center ice, and we slashed each other with such force that we both had the wind knocked out of us.

I remember thinking, *Holy Jesus, this guy is solid as a rock*.

What people don't understand about Swedish players is that, even though they aren't fighters, they are as tough as Canadian players. They can take a beating and they won't ever go away. They will use their stick and they will stand up for themselves. I learned that from playing with, and against, Swedish players.

The rivalry pushed both the Avalanche and Red Wings to be the best teams we could be. Without us, there is no them—and without them, there is no us. It felt like war when we played the Avalanche, but we respected their warrior mentality.

We also respected the Carolina Hurricanes, who were our Stanley Cup Final opponent in 2002. The media believed it would be a walkover because the Hurricanes had finished with 25 fewer points than us in the regular season. But the Hurricanes had also been underdogs in their three previous series, and yet somehow had found a way to win.

Before the Stanley Cup Final began, Carolina coach Paul Maurice even joked that he was applying for "underdog status" because he believed his team played better when critics didn't give them much of a chance. He lovingly referred to his players as "mongrels."

We didn't take the Hurricanes lightly, and they showed us in Game 1 why we shouldn't. Ron Francis scored 58 seconds into overtime to give Carolina a 3–2 win in the opener in Detroit. Twice, we had a lead in that game and could not hold it.

Game 2 was a different story. We won 3–1 to tie the series heading to Raleigh, North Carolina, for Games 3 and 4. It was Game 3 that decided the series, and honestly we almost lost that game.

Hullie scored with 1:14 remaining in regulation to tie the game, and we didn't win it until Igor Larionov scored at 14:47 of the third overtime.

There was plenty of angst for our team in overtime because the Hurricanes were a confident bunch. At that point, they were 7–1 in overtime games on the season. Their goaltender Arturs Irbe was 7–0 in overtime games. Meanwhile, we had lost four out of five overtime games, including the first game of that series.

At the time, the game ended up being the third-longest Stanley Cup Final game ever played. Again, Hasek was terrific in net, making 41 saves, including 22 in overtime.

Larionov, who was 41 then, had scored earlier in the game to become the oldest player ever to score in a Stanley Cup Final.

We ended up winning Game 4 by a score of 3–0 to take charge of the series. But it would have been a completely different series had Carolina been able to win Game 3. That building was as loud as it gets. They would have been overflowing with momentum in Game 4 had they beat us in Game 3.

That's why I say that series was closer than people realize, even though we won it in five games.

We won the clinching game by a score of 3–1. Scotty announced his retirement on the ice while we were celebrating.

When I look back at that championship, what I think about is how we came back from a 2–0 deficit to win the opening round series against Vancouver. The media thought we were dead at that point.

Before Game 3 in that series, Yzerman addressed the team. It wasn't a fiery oration. It wasn't like Herb Brooks addressing his American players before the game against the Soviets in 1980. It was Stevie being Stevie. He said that we were better than the way we had been playing. He said we needed to relax and play the way we know how to play. He said we needed to take charge.

The reason why Yzerman's address was important was *because* he decided to address us. I can only remember him making about three major captain's speeches. So when he spoke, we listened. We went out and won four consecutive games against the Canucks.

But we were more inspired by Yzerman's actions than his words. He led us to that championship while playing on one leg. The cartilage in his right knee was shredded. He couldn't practice. Not long after winning in 2002, Steve had to have an osteotomy, a surgical procedure where a bone is cut to realign the knee. A shim was inserted underneath the knee to remove pressure from the hinge. That surgery is usually done on senior citizens to give them mobility in their later years.

Even we didn't know the extent of Yzerman's knee damage during the 2002 playoffs. We just knew that he looked like he was in more pain than anyone we had seen.

He never complained. He just showed up every day, took a needle to deaden the pain, and then went out and played.

Yzerman basically refused to even acknowledge that there was a problem.

"How're you doing, Steve?" I would ask.

"I'm fine," he'd say.

Sometimes he'd change it up and just say "Good" when you asked him how he was feeling. To Steve, that was a comprehensive medical report.

Doctors would try to time the administering of the needle to give Yzerman the maximum amount of relief during a game. But if the game went to overtime, the relief would wear off.

It didn't truly hit me how debilitating his injury was until I watched him try to pull himself off the ice during the Stanley Cup Final. He had gotten hit in the corner, and had to use his stick to support his weight to will himself back to his feet. It was painful to watch how long it took him to get back on his skates.

Another powerful memory of that playoff run centers on how amazing Hasek was. He played 23 games and posted six shutouts. At one point in the Stanley Cup Final, Hasek went 166 minutes without allowing Carolina to score a goal.

The first Stanley Cup was special because it ended a 42-year drought in Detroit. And it was special because I scored the clinching goals. The second championship was special because we won it for Vladimir Konstantinov and Sergei Mnatsakanov.

But the 2002 championship was important for a variety of reasons. It was memorable because we helped Robitaille, Hasek, Fredrik Olausson, and Steve Duchesne win their first Cups.

People tend to forget that Olausson and Duchesne played a big role on that team. In Game 3 of the Stanley Cup Final, Duchesne lost a handful of teeth when he was struck in the face with a shot. When I saw the aftermath of that injury, Duchesne looked like the famous old photo of Bobby Clarke smiling without any fucking front teeth. Duchesne wasn't even fazed by his need for dentistry. He was quickly back in the game, and his pass triggered the rush that led to Larionov's winning goal.

The win in 2002 was also extra meaningful because it had been four years since our last Stanley Cup championship.

That gave us three championships in a six-year span, which certainly helped us make a case for being one of the great NHL teams. It was also memorable because it was Bowman's ninth Stanley Cup championship, breaking a tie with his mentor, Toe Blake, for most NHL coaching championships.

One of the best moments of my NHL career came while I was celebrating that 2002 championship. Red Wings owners Mike and Marian Ilitch threw a party at their home, and I was standing near one of the buffet tables, munching on shrimp, when Scotty unexpectedly walked up to me and started talking.

Scotty wasn't the easiest coach to play for because he was demanding. But I enjoyed playing for him because he made me feel wanted. Plus, I felt he cared about my well-being.

That was made clear to me one night playing St. Louis when Tony Twist was trying to goad me into a second fight. I really didn't want to fight Twist. Nobody really wanted to fight Twist, because we all understood that he could hurt you.

Seeing that both of us were jawing before a faceoff, Scotty stood on the bench and screamed, "If you fight Twist again, you will never play another minute for me."

I turned to Twist and said, "Sorry Twister, but I want to play. Can't fight you."

Thank you Scotty for saving my ass. He knew exactly what he was doing when he yelled me. He was helping me save face.

When Scotty talks, words fly out of his mouth like quick machine gun bursts, and you can never be sure of his aim.

"One thing I never did in my career is tell my players how much I appreciated them," Bowman said to me that night at the Ilitches'.

Now that Bowman was retired, he was totally comfortable talking to his players.

"I just want you to know that you're my second-favorite right wing next to Guy Lafleur," Bowman blurted out. "I hope you aren't mad."

The greatest coach in NHL history just told me that he liked no right winger better than me except 560-goal scorer Lafluer.

No, I'm not mad at taking a backseat to Lafleur. That was a pretty fucking amazing moment in my career. I'm not a Hall of Famer, but that was my Hall of Fame moment.

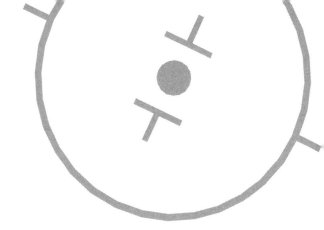

Chapter 9

Grinder

"Hey, hey, I wanna be a rockstar"

—"Rockstar"
Nickelback

Grinder

When I was playing hockey for the Detroit Red Wings while at the same time performing in my rock band Grinder, I felt like I was living every man's double-career fantasy.

How many males in North America would love to be living a life where they can claim to be both a professional athlete and a rock 'n' roller? Those days when scoring goals was my day job and writing tunes was my side job certainly were among the best times of my life.

In 2005, Grinder played for 12,000 people at the Arts, Beats, and Eats Festival in Pontiac, Michigan, and I remember looking out over the crowd and feeling the same rush of emotion that I experienced in a playoff hockey game.

You hear frequently of athletes wanting to take the stage as musicians, and I think it's because they know they can find the same adrenaline surge they enjoyed in their sporting endeavors.

Former Detroit Red Wings player Boyd Devereaux is an accomplished guitarist, and he contacted me after my retirement about putting together a band of former athletes, which I think is an idea that could work. I think fans want to see athletes in a different environment, and I think there are plenty of athletes who would love to find a new place to grab the spotlight.

As a hockey player, I had to maintain a steady flow of pure energy for the length of a 45-second shift. As a band member, you have to maintain a high level of focus and emotion for a much longer duration. It feels like you are on a never-ending shift because you know you have to keep the crowd entertained. I love that feeling.

The first time I witnessed people in an audience singing the words to a song that I wrote, I thought it was the coolest feeling I'd ever known.

We formed the band Grinder in 1997 to do the song "Step Outside" to help raise money for Sergei Mnatsakanov and Vladimir Konstantinov after they were injured severely in the 1997 limousine accident.

Grinder included guitarists Billy Reedy and Eli Ruhf, bassist James Anders, and drummer Eric Miller. The group performed under the name Novadriver when I was not around.

The guys in the band jokingly called me "Mac Jagger."

The "Step Outside" cut appeared on the tribute album *Believing in Detroit: A Tribute to Vladdy and Sergei.* After it was recorded, we were all very proud of it. Today, I think it is lame. I have learned so much more about music since then, mostly through my friendship with bandmate, James Anders.

He was the heart, soul, and musical inspiration of Grinder. We would sit around for hours talking about what makes good music. He schooled me on the importance of Iggy Pop and the Stooges and Jim Morrison and the Doors and lots of others.

Grinder was alive, in various forms, from 1997 to about 2006, and we made two albums. I'd estimate we performed live approximately 120 times.

"Our music is stripped down rock 'n' roll with a little bit of punk," I told *Sports Illustrated* in 2005.

There was a Nirvana influence as well, and certainly some MC5 influence.

The Detroit Red Wings never truly understood how important the band was to me. They viewed it as a distraction to my hockey career, and it probably was. I was very serious about my efforts to make Grinder a successful band. I believed I could do both jobs well. Every time I stepped on the ice, I gave it all that I had. But when I was off the ice, I wanted to think about music, not hockey.

The band certainly received our share of attention. The media liked the story of an NHL enforcer being involved in a rock band. MTV even did a story on us. I liked the business of rock 'n' roll.

I never had any delusions about my ability as a musician. I was not a natural. I would never be a candidate to win *American Idol* or sing opera. I knew a couple of chords on the guitar. But what I had was an intense desire to improve, and I did improve. I received some voice coaching, and I worked at my new craft. I listened to how others did it, and by the end of Grinder's run I could get the job done as a vocalist. I could hold an audience.

"I can hold a tune and not butcher it," is how I phrased it during a 2003 interview with MTV.

I've always felt I had some ability to use words to express my feelings. I could write poetry when I was young. I found that I liked songwriting. I feel as if I have some talent in that area.

Grinder enjoyed some incredible moments, such as the time that famed Stooges guitarist Ron Asheton came on stage and played with us at the Blind Pig in Ann Arbor, Michigan. He has since passed away.

We also had the privilege of having MC5 bassist Michael Smith perform with us on stage. He also has died since then.

As a rock 'n' roll fan my entire life, I was like a kid living in a fantasy world. The first time I met Dave Grohl of the Foo Fighters, I had a man-crush on him. I was almost speechless. He had been with Nirvana before the Foo Fighters and I considered myself a huge fan of his work.

Mike Mouyianis was Grinder's manager, and he and I were escorted backstage at Cobo Hall just 45 minutes before Grohl took the stage.

It was almost uncomfortable for me to be there because they were all getting ready to perform. Not surprising, they were listening to music.

When you are in that situation, your greatest fear is that your idol will not be the person who you think he is. You don't want your bubble burst. But Grohl turned out to be even more gracious than I had hoped he would be.

He asked me to pick a song for the guys to hear before they went on stage. "What kind of music do you like?" he asked.

It was an amazing moment for me to have with someone I admired.

After my stepfather Craig died in 1999, we used some of our appearances in the early years of Grinder to help raise money for the

McCarty Foundation, a charity founded to honor my stepfather's fight against multiple myeloma.

The band lost some momentum after 2000, but I was re-energized by singing on stage with Kid Rock at the Jefferson Beach Marina after the Red Wings won the Stanley Cup in 2002. I have a great photo of Devereaux and I on stage with the Kid.

I remember telling Jim Anders, "We should put the band back together."

It was like the Eagles reuniting; I jumped back in with both feet. I rented out space in an industrial park in Warren, Michigan, and turned it into our sound-proof rehearsal hall.

It was really like our Bat Cave. I bought a pool table, and we had a bedroom and a bar. I'm not going to lie to you—it was a party house, and I stayed there too many nights.

This is when we made the transformation from bar band to concert band. I bought a 40-foot tricked-out recreational vehicle. It was a sweet ride.

My estimate is that I spent around $400,000 to set up the band for what I believed was an attempt to take it to another level.

Grinder had some incredibly fun times.

Grinder's most important man behind the scenes was Tim Drummond. He runs his own sound company out of Bay City, Michigan, called Hyperman. We stuck him with the nickname "Hyperdude."

He did our sound for a gig in Bay City and I was so impressed that I asked him to work exclusively for us.

He soon became the most important member of our band because he handled sound, driving, cooking, and security. Don't be fooled by his long-haired rock look. Drummond is immensely qualified to handle security because he is a former Navy seal.

To kill time on long road trips in the RV, Anders came up with a game called "What can Tim kill you with and how?"

The rules were simple: When it was your turn, you had to come up with an item and Tim would have to say whether it was possible, with his training, to kill you with that item.

Tim had to answer in five to 10 seconds. For example, someone would say: "Paper clip," and Drummond would say: "Open it and jam it in your artery."

Someone would say: "Sharpie pen" and Drummond would answer: "Jam it up your nose and into your brain."

We would play this game, on and off, for hours. There would be lulls, times when the bus would go quiet, and then someone would offer up a potential murder weapon for Drummond to review.

It was a fun game. One time, Drummond was on a roll, offering up his clever strategies for murder, when Anders yells that he had a possible stumper.

"Dude, I got a good one," Anders said. "A bag of potato chips."

"Empty or full?" Drummond asked instantly in his military tone.

Everyone in the bus laughed uncontrollably for several minutes. We were all laughing so hard that no one heard how he could kill us with a full or empty potato chip bag.

That may have been the night that we all realized that Drummond could kill us all without much trouble.

Drummond remains my friend today, and when we are together he still looks after me. My wife, Sheryl, calls him "Houdini" because whenever crowds become uncomfortable at autograph sessions or appearances he can make us disappear in a hurry.

Our first album, *Gotta Keep Movin'*, by Red Line Records, came out in 2003. It featured five original songs, plus two covers, "Neat, Neat, Neat" by the Damned and "No Fun" by Iggy Pop and the Stooges.

It was recorded at the Chophouse, the recording studio owned by Kid Rock.

Our stage appearances included shows at the Silverdome in Pontiac and the Masonic Temple in Detroit. Grinder was also featured at the tailgate party as part of the Jim Rome World Tour stop at the Palace at Auburn Hills.

One of my favorite musical moments actually came on a small stage in a Moscow night club when I was with the Detroit players who went over to play in Igor Larionov's charity game. Kid Rock made the trip with us, and we went up on stage with him and sang Lynyrd Skynyrd's "Sweet Home Alabama."

The NHL lockout of 2004–05 gave us our first opportunity to expand our horizons. Grinder had an 80-venue tour that included stops in Detroit, Chicago, Los Angeles, and Las Vegas.

We drove our "bus" for 34 consecutive hours to play at the famed Roxy in Los Angeles.

The tour was a critical success because it gained us some notoriety and more of a national following. But it ended up costing me money. I fronted the money for the trip, and I paid the expenses and wages that the tour revenue didn't cover. At every stop, I was there handing out the meal money and money to bum around. (I had to put everyone on a gambling allowance in Vegas.)

But I would do it all over again because I loved the romance of touring with a rock 'n' roll band.

Playing music was always therapeutic for me. To be honest, I might be in worse shape today if not for music. Songwriting helped me explore my feelings; it helped me comes to grips with my thoughts about my addiction, my life, and my family.

My favorite Grinder piece is I song I wrote called "Be Me." It's about what I was feeling about my life. It's still true today. Here are the lyrics:

Why can't I be what I wanna be? with attitude, no apology, without compromise, it's my life, you can say what you wanna say, put me down if it makes your day, in the end, what you see is what you get.

You look at me and you only see what you wanna see, I'm just a man and I wanna be, just wanna be me.

Don't want your rules or your social machine, you criticize me for playing the scene but look hard and you'll see you're a lot like me, I live my life the American dream, but underneath it's not always serene, in the end no regrets no mystery.

You look at me and you only see what you wanna see, I'm just a man and I wanna be, just wanna be me. Just wanna be me, just wanna be me, just wanna be me.

Why can't I be what I wanna be, don't want your rules or conservative dreams, no politics or conformity, a casualty of society, in the end, what you see is what you get.

You look at me and you only see what you wanna see, I'm just a man and I'm playing the scene, I'm not a machine, you look at me and you only see what you wanna see, I'm just a man, I WANNA BE ME, just wanna be me, just wanna be me, just wanna be me, just wanna be me.

You have to reflect your personal experiences in your music. I also like our song "Shooting Star," which is about the foolishness of believing your own hype and expecting fame to last forever.

A sample of the lyrics: "You're a shooting star, living for today, no matter who you are, you always fade away."

When I was asked recently if I have any regrets about Grinder, my answer was, "Yes, my regret is James Anders died."

I don't really regret any aspect of my association with Grinder. I wish the band was still alive today. Yes, I should have been more frugal when it came to funding the band. It was a costly venture for me financially.

How much money did we pour into the gas tank of that RV to get to our tour stops? It was a drain to be sure.

I actually did receive some of my money back for the RV because there was an electrical fire on it while the band was driving back from up North. I was not on that trip, but it burned out while band members were pulling our equipment off it. Insurance provided a settlement, although certainly not what I paid for it.

But the music died for us when James Anders died. He was only 40 years old, and he died suddenly, while he was on the phone with his wife. It was a heart ailment that had gone undetected.

I still miss him today. Conversations with him fueled my passion for music. Every time we talked I understood music more. We wrote songs together. He had music in his soul. He died in May 2005, right after we produced our second album, *Out of Our Heads*.

We soldiered on because he would have wanted us to continue to play the music. That was the proper way to honor his memory. But it was not the same after he died. The band came to Calgary to perform after I signed with the Flames. But we haven't performed since 2006.

I'm sure people in the hockey world still believe that my interest in music was a negative for my career. One of the unspoken rules is that athletes are supposed to concentrate solely on their careers to the exclusion of all other endeavors. More than one of my teammates asked me to dial back on my music career because they sensed that the Red Wings were growing weary of my musical escapades.

It may surprise people to know that when the NHL lockout occurred in 2004, I was far more interested in music than I was in hockey.

At that time, if I could have made enough money to support myself in music, I would have gladly given up my NHL career. I was burned out on hockey. At that point, I would have been ready to turn the page.

Chapter 10

Goodbye, Detroit

"Sometimes goodbye is a second chance"

—"Second Chance"
Shinedown

Goodbye, Detroit

Imagine the furor I would have created had I signed with the Colorado Avalanche in 2006. That was a possibility after the Red Wings bought out my contract that summer.

I don't think the Detroit fan base would have ever forgiven me had I chosen that option.

It would be like President Obama saying he was going to join the Republican Party or Ford Motor Company announcing that it was moving its headquarters to Japan.

But after the Red Wings announced that they were buying out Derian Hatcher, Ray Whitney, and me, the Avalanche were the first team to show interest in signing me. The team's director of player personnel was Brad Smith, an ex–Red Wings player who was nicknamed "Motor City Smitty." In that era, he scouted many games at Joe Louis Arena and he told me he had an appreciation of what I offered to a team.

Although I had hoped to spend my entire career as a Red Wing, I wasn't angry with Detroit general manager Ken Holland's decision to buy out my contract because I knew it was a logical move.

The Red Wings had a payroll of about $77 million in 2003–04, and then owners locked out players because they wanted a salary cap. We lost the 2004–05 season, and then we ended up with a $39 million salary cap. The Red Wings had to trim their payroll, and they had a six-day window to buy out players without having the buyout count against the cap.

In buying out Hatcher ($4.66 million), Whitney ($2.66 million), and me ($1.7 million), they cut almost $9 million.

If I were the Detroit general manager, I would have made the same decision that Holland made. If I were making less than $1 million, I might have been mad that the Red Wings didn't work harder to keep me. But by that time in my career, I was making real money.

Plus, I was 33 and I had been injured for a large chunk of the previous season. When you're that age, you're always vulnerable.

Even though the moves made perfect sense, it was still difficult for Holland to tell me that I was no longer going to be a Red Wing. He and I had been together in the organization for 11 years. He was my boss, but to me he seemed more like a father figure. Because it's my personality to do whatever I can to help the team, I tried to make the conversation as easy as possible.

I told him at the meeting that there were no hard feelings, and that I understood that the team was forced into this move by factors that were out of Holland's control.

As I look back on that situation, I blame myself for putting myself in the position of being one of the cuts when the team needed to trim.

At that point in my career, the Red Wings were not overly pleased with some of my off-ice habits. They knew that I had a drug issue, and that my marriage was breaking up. They probably worried that a divorce would mean even less stability in my life and maybe wilder behavior.

Also, Holland and some of my teammates had asked me to be less involved with my band, Grinder. The argument was that it had become a distraction, and that it had taken my focus away from hockey.

Holland wanted me not to have any gigs during the season, and he wasn't happy when he showed up at training camp and discovered we were playing in Traverse City to take advantage of all of the Red Wings fans that were in town.

The point is that perhaps the Red Wings would have been more creative in trying to find a way to keep me if I had been a model citizen.

I wasn't shocked by the buyout, because there was media speculation about the situation long before it happened. I was surprised and pleased when I received a call from Calgary general manager and coach Darryl Sutter because I had always respected the Sutter family approach to hockey.

He offered me $800,000 a season on a two-year deal, and frankly I would have gone there for less.

I thought Sutter would be the perfect coach for me, and that turned out to be the case. He never gave me any specific instructions on how to play, other than to say I should play the way I always had.

Based on how Sutter treated me, I believed he respected what I had to offer as a player. That's all I ever ask from my coach. I just want to feel like I'm contributing. He had some similarities to Scotty Bowman. Both men were tough coaches, but they'd adjusted their styles through the years to accommodate the changes in the game and the players.

Sutter put me on a line with Stephane Yelle and Marcus Nilson and we stayed together most of the season.

Maybe we weren't the second coming of the Grind Line, but we had good chemistry. We were effective. Yelle was called "Sandbox" because he did all the dirty work. I knew Yelle from playing against him when he was in Colorado, but I gained even more for him as a teammate. He sweats the small stuff, and he was always willing to do the little things that make a team successful.

It was a good group in Calgary, and it helped me that recovering alcoholic Chris Simon was on the team. At the team gatherings, I wasn't the only one not drinking. Simon understood my struggles maybe even better than I did. We went to meetings together, and he had been fighting alcoholism even longer than I had.

I'm sure some of my teammates knew bits and pieces of my battles with substance abuse, but no one really asked me about it in-depth. Simon knew details, but he was not the kind of guy who was going to talk to anyone else about it. Chris was a quality guy.

The two of us had some fun acting as chauffeurs for goalie Miikka Kiprusoff, who rates as one of the funniest teammates I've ever had.

He smoked and drank Scotch, and I swear the more he drank the better his English got. If you could understand him perfectly, you knew he probably had had too much to drink.

Kiprusoff reminded me a bit of Chris Osgood because we would be at a gathering and he wouldn't say much for a long period of time and then suddenly he would make a random off-the-wall comment that would leave the room in stitches.

On the ice, he was like Dominik Hasek in that he didn't like to get beat—even in practice.

What I remember most about the Flames is what a fun-loving group we had that season.

The boys always enjoyed watching Mixed Martial Arts (MMA) on TV, usually at Rhett Warrener's or Jarome Iginla's homes. They especially loved Chuck Liddell's fights.

Those nights always seemed like a frat party. Once everyone had been into the sauce for a while, the shirts would come off and the wrestling would commence.

Iginla always squared off against his best buddy, Chuck Kobasew, and it would always end up getting out of hand. Some of us would have to step in and serve as peacemakers.

It was like the battles that Draper and I used to have, except we didn't have an audience. It was like the Roman circus when Iginla and Kobasew put on a match for their teammates' enjoyment.

We actually banned MMA watching during the playoffs because we were afraid that someone might get hurt.

By the way, Warrener is one of the best teammates I ever had in my career. He instantly reminded me of Chris Chelios because of the way he treated everyone. Those two players treated all of their teammates the same, whether they had been with them for 30 days or 10 seasons. Warrener took care of everyone on the Flames, in the same manner that Chelios took care of everyone on the Red Wings. If you needed a hook-up for anything in Calgary, Warrener was the man who could get it done.

One of my favorite memories of my Calgary days was the Bad Christmas Sweater party Warrener hosted. I saw some of the gaudiest Christmas sweaters known to man. I recall Yelle won the hideous sweater contest wearing one with a butt-ugly reindeer on the front. Honestly, it looked like that reindeer was going to leap off his chest.

Warrener had gone all out for this party. He had a nice place with a beautiful open kitchen. He had his Christmas tree all lit up and beautifully trimmed in the true holiday spirit.

Everyone brought their wives or girlfriends, and everyone was dolled up for the occasion. It had all of the ingredients of a classy affair.

However, the Calgary boys did like to drink at their parties. That meant it was inevitable that a food fight was going to break out at this holiday gathering.

This wasn't two kids at a breakfast table hurling Cheerios at one another. This was a holiday spread food fight, complete with turkey, mashed potatoes, stuffing, cranberries, and corn, among other items.

The second ammunition dump included a table of cupcakes in the corner that also came with a chocolate fondue fountain.

Also available were bottles and bottles of red wine, quality wine that could stain carpeting, with no remorse or remedy.

Trying to figure out who started this food fight is like trying to figure out who really caused World War I. Fingers were pointed at many different parties. Clearly, entangling alliances played a major role. Once the first shot was fired, emotion simply took over.

My recollection is that Warrener, because he owned the house, was comfortable enough to throw the first cupcake at defenseman Robyn Regehr.

But I may be saying that because Warrener and Regehr were usually involved at the start of all the horseplay that got out of hand. As soon as Regehr was hit, it became a night of mass destruction.

It was the mother of all food fights. I remember ducking a mashed potato bomb and then getting drilled in the chest with a chocolate-frosted missile. Turkey explosions were landing everywhere. No one was safe. Players. Wives. Girlfriends. There were 30 people involved in the skirmish. Casualties were high.

At one point, Warrener fell into the Christmas tree and knocked it over, probably because he was trying to avoid a barrage of salad raining down on him.

When a cease-fire was called 15 minutes after the war began, Warrener's house looked like it had been under a mortar attack. People were trying to scrape chocolate out of their eyes, and sweep the cranberry sauce off their dresses and shirts. Women were pulling turkey remnants out of blouses. Carpets were stained blood-red. Clothing was ruined. Many people had vegetables and/or stuffing in their hair. You couldn't put your hand down without it landing in a goo that used to be dinner. Everyone was sticky. Everyone was drunk.

It may have been the best holiday party I ever attended. No one is ever going to forget that gathering, particularly Warrener, who said it took him three days to clean up the mess.

But knowing Warrener, if he had it to over again, he would have done it exactly the same way.

This was a tight team. We called Regehr "Reggie." He was the king of the iPod, and he and I spent many nights watching rock shows at the Back Alley. I liked the young guys on that team as well. Chuck Kobasew, Matt Lombardi, and Byron Ritchie, in particular, were respectful kids. What I remember most about the Flames is that we held at least one team party per month.

The move to Calgary was also good for me because it allowed me to become more acquainted with my biological father, Doug Francottie, who lived in Edmonton. I'd reached out to him in 1996, but I wasn't ready then to stay in touch with him. I believed I was ready to meet him in 2004, mostly because I needed answers to the question of why I was the way I was.

I was 32 when I met my father for the first time. It was on a Red Wings road trip to Edmonton. We talked for six hours. He said the reason he never had any contact with me was because he was in the Witness Protection Program. While he was working as a cop in British Columbia he took down an Asian mob boss and the department decided he needed to enter the Program to protect his family. It reminded me of the story I told women to get rid of them after I grew bored with an affair.

"It's the best thing for you," I would say. "It's not your fault. It's my fault. I'm leaving you to protect you from me."

My biological father's explanation sounded as hollow as my speeches must have sounded to the women I bedded.

Doug Francottie said once it was determined that the threat to his life was over, he came out of hiding, although he still remains a bit secretive even today.

In the two years I was in Calgary, Doug came down often to hang out with me.

He told me he had been following my hockey career for years. He'd even seen me play NHL games live before he actually met me.

I don't know whether I believed every word he told me, but getting to know him was important to me because it helped me understand why I am the way I am. It took me reconnecting with him to realize that what was going on inside of him was what was going on inside of me. I've recently heard Bishop T.D. Jakes say, "The problems were generational, not situational." And that's exactly correct. It is painfully clear that he and I have some of the same wiring.

He's also an alcoholic. His drink is Bacardi and Diet Coke. We spent a lot of time together in casinos. My father was constantly being chased by bill collectors. He seems to have many of the same issues that I have, leading me to the conclusion that I inherited some, if not all, of my demons from him.

We kept in contact for a while, but I eventually realized that I was initiating most of our meetings. He also left out pertinent details to his life story, such as the fact that he had a second family. We fell out of contact. He was in Windsor two years ago, and tried to reach out to me. I attempted to call him back, but by then his number was disconnected.

When Bob Probert died, I arrived in Windsor at the funeral to find my father standing in the parking lot. He said he knew I would be there, and he wanted to see me. We talked briefly, and I haven't seen him since. I don't know where he is today.

When I played with Calgary that first season, Simon and I shared the tough-guy duties. He had eight fights and I had seven, plus one more in the postseason against Anaheim's Sean O'Donnell.

Sutter played me about 11 minutes per game during the regular season, and I ended up with seven goals and six assists for 13 points. He seemed happy with the way I was playing. I never had a single issue with Sutter.

In the playoffs, I ended up scoring two goals in our seven-game-series loss to the Anaheim Ducks. One of my goals came in overtime in the opening game.

In a 1–1 game, teammate Kristian Huselius, stationed behind the net, spotted me and fed me a perfect pass as I cruised into the slot. I one-timed the puck past goalie Ilya Bryzgalov for the victory. What made that moment such an amazing coincidence was the fact that almost a decade before I had been on the ice with the young teenage puck magician Huselius at the Tomas Storm hockey camp.

That's the beauty of NHL playoff hockey. On a team full of guys with more offensive skill than me, the role player was the guy who produced the game-winning goal.

In my exit interview it was clear that the Flames were pleased with me and were looking forward to having me back the following season. I looked forward to coming back because I enjoyed playing for Sutter. He coached the game the way I liked to play the game.

When Sutter coached the Los Angeles Kings to the Stanley Cup championship in 2012, I certainly wasn't surprised. I could tell that the Kings were buying into the Sutter program. Guys want to play hard for Sutter. They want to win for him because he treats them like men.

I was optimistic about my future with the Flames. At the time, what I didn't realize was that Sutter would not be back behind the Flames bench. I also could not have predicted that my struggles with substance abuse would hit an all-time low.

When the Flames announced on July 12 that Sutter was stepping down as coach but would remain as general manager, I had no idea how it would change my status in Calgary.

To be honest, I didn't care what was happening in Calgary because I was in the midst of a drunken stupor.

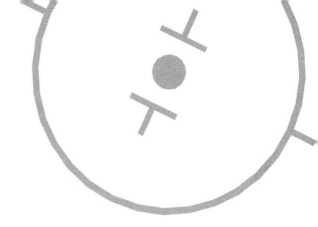

Chapter 11

Falling Down in Hawaii

"Well if I have one I'll have 13, now there ain't no in between, 'cause the more I drink the more I drink"

—"The More I Drink"
Blake Shelton

Falling Down in Hawaii

Alcoholics don't need a reason to drink. They need a reason not to drink. By 2006, I had gone 10 years without drinking. But I woke up one morning in Hawaii and decided I needed to drink two beers and a mini-bar bottle of Patron Silver Tequila.

I don't know why. I have absolutely no idea.

Maybe it was because the sky looked blue or the moon was going to be full that night or the beaches looked spectacular. Maybe my life was going too fucking well.

There's never really a true explanation for why an addict tumbles off the wagon. To explain why I resumed drinking after a period of not drinking, I usually say that I contracted a case of the I-don't-give-a-fucks.

Eight Calgary players and their wives had gone to Hawaii after the season, and while we were there I went up to my hotel room and decided to drink.

I didn't stop.

The next day, I went with my Flames teammates and their wives and girlfriends on a tour boat with an open bar. Jarome Iginla, Marcus Nilson, Byron Ritchie, Robyn Regehr, Tony Amonte, Rhett Warrener, and Stephane Yelle were among the players who were in attendance. I was with my girlfriend, Anna Okuszko, a woman I had met in Calgary.

I drank heavily. Probably everyone noticed, but no one said anything, mostly because my Calgary teammates didn't have a grasp of the seriousness of my problem. Chris Simon wasn't on the trip, and he knew the most because he had gone to Alcoholics Anonymous meetings with me in Calgary.

My Flames teammates knew I wasn't drinking, but they'd only known me for one season. That means we had about eight months together. They didn't know the depths of my problem. Even if they suspected I was in trouble, they didn't have enough history with me to confront me in a meaningful way.

If this had happened when I was playing with the Red Wings, Kris Draper or Kirk Maltby or Chris Osgood or Steve Yzerman or someone would have tried to intervene. They probably would have failed, but they would have tried. You can't stop an addict from drinking when he or she wants to drink.

Even Anna didn't know my history because I had purposely kept it from her. I wasn't Mr. Communication when it came to my problems.

Just to be clear, I had not been clean for 10 years when I had those drinks in Hawaii. The trip to my hotel room simply ended a 10-year abstinence from *booze*.

After I had stopped drinking, I initially stayed completely sober for three years. Then I started doing drugs after my stepfather died. I had an ecstasy problem for a while, and then got off that. But after 1999 I was never willing to give up marijuana, an issue that I will discuss later in the book. I smoked pot regularly after 1999. There is no question that I was more in control when I occasionally smoked pot than I was when I drank regularly.

Once I resumed drinking, it didn't take long for me to spin out of control with my alcohol use. After the trip to Hawaii, I went back to Detroit and then I headed to Las Vegas to party.

I flew Anna to Las Vegas, though I thought we were close to breaking up. I was having a great time in Vegas and we were winning at the casinos. But Anna clearly wasn't happy.

"Well, then, why don't we get married?" I said.

I was totally wasted at the time. My drunken logic was that it would be less painful to marry her than to break up with her.

Because I was winning at the table, I had a wad of cash and we went to the jewelry store and I bought her a diamond ring. Honestly, I can't be sure because I was drunk at the time, but I recall that the ring cost $20,000.

We were married at a Las Vegas chapel the next day. Two of her friends were witnesses, and there was no one else there. Even the guy I went to Vegas with didn't come.

My hangover was debilitating to the point that I couldn't even go to dinner after the ceremony. I had to return to the hotel to sleep it off.

This could have been a scene from the movie *The Hangover,* only I was doing the crazy shit instead of actor Ed Helms.

When I saw *The Hangover* in 2009, the events of the bachelor party didn't seem quite as unbelievable. If you drink enough booze, you can wake up anywhere and find out that your life has changed dramatically.

The symbol of my fall was a trip to New York City for Ozzfest on July 29, 2006. The Ozzfest is a yearly heavy metal music festival that tours the United States.

I went there with two friends from Calgary, and I planned to be at the festival for one day. Instead, my Ozzfest stay lasted almost two weeks.

Sobriety didn't make the trip with me.

My primary reason to attend Ozzfest was to see Black Label Society, the band headlined by lead vocalist and guitarist Zakk Wylde. He was formerly the guitarist for Ozzy Osbourne and he is known as one of the best guitarists the world has ever produced.

The events of what happened are somewhat foggy, but the escapade started when a New York City cop working security for Black Label Society recognized me. He was a New York Rangers fan.

"No fuckin' way! It's Darren fuckin' McCarty!" he said in his Brooklyn accent.

One thing led to another, and we ended up backstage, where we hooked up with the band's bass player, Johnny "JD" DeServio, who is a New Jersey Devils fan.

We ended up drinking together, and after too much booze to measure, DeServio says, "Shit, we're heading to Hartford next. Why don't you jump on the tour bus and join us?"

My buddies had to return to Calgary. But to me, being asked to be a roadie for Black Label Society was like being asked to play in an All-Star Game. You would never refuse that invitation.

I ended up being a roadie for five days, and I did everything a roadie does, including moving equipment and making sure band members had what they needed to put on a show.

Wylde used laminated-lyrics cards during the concert, and one of my jobs was going out and replacing them as the show progressed. I would be running out on stage with 10,000-plus screaming fans watching me. In that respect, it was just like playing a hockey game.

We also drank heavily. I remember one particular night when we stopped at a Hooters and the drinking put me over the edge. The drinkers included a cop/bodyguard named Phil and Zakk's brother-in-law, Mark, who was the tour manager. They challenged Zakk and me to a beer-pitcher-chugging competition.

The beer of choice for the competition was Guinness Stout. That's like dueling with long knives. There's no margin for error when you're chugging stout.

The competition lasted through six pitchers, and we found out later that Mark was cheating by going into the bathroom and throwing up after each round.

My puking didn't come until a little bit later. On the tour bus, I crawled from the carpeted lounge area to the linoleum-floored kitchen area and puked everywhere.

The next memory I have is waking up on the tour bus, lying on a comfy couch with my head on a pillow. A blanket was covering me.

Needing to piss, I forced myself off the couch and discovered Zakk Wylde, the greatest guitarist in the world, sleeping on the floor below me with no pillow and no blanket. It was like he was my devoted dog watching over me.

"You all right, man?" he asked.

"Yes," I said. "Dude, thanks for taking care of me."

"No problem," he said. "We never leave a man behind."

After five days, I left BLS. But by then I had hooked up with the band System of a Down, a California-based rock band also known as SOAD. I was just a tag-along with this group. I just drank, got high, and soaked in what it was like to be a rocker on the road. After a week of partying like a rock star, I literally jumped off the bus in Washington, D.C., and flew home.

During my entire 12 days away, I never called anyone at home. No one had any real idea where I was or what I was doing.

Poor Anna had no idea what she had signed up for when she married me.

When I returned home to Detroit, my mother; my sister, Melissa; and my ex-wife, Cheryl, staged an intervention at the Grinder Bat Cave in Warren.

I knew it was coming. As I mentioned earlier, watching Bob Probert's downfall had taught me how far I could push the envelope. He showed me the line that shouldn't be crossed, even though he crossed it often.

Throughout my career, I always recognized when I was at the edge of the cliff. Subconsciously, that may be the reason why I embarked on my music-fest bender. I probably needed one wild-ass escapade before returning to the world of responsible behavior.

My family convinced me to go to Hazelden in Minnesota, for a five-week rehabilitation program. It was my third trip to rehab. "Going off to summer camp," I told my buddies.

What that meant was that I was going to be late for training camp, and I also wasn't going to be in great shape. But at least I was going to be clean and sober.

I played it straight with the Flames. I called president and CEO Ken King and Darryl Sutter and explained my situation. Both of them assured me that my decision to enter rehabilitation wouldn't impact my status with the team. They told me I had made the right decision. I entered rehab feeling positive about the fact that it would not have a negative impact on my career.

It seemed like there would be a seamless transition between playing for Sutter and playing for Jim Playfair, because Playfair had been Sutter's assistant. He knew all of us, and I presumed he would see the same value in each of us that Sutter saw. My presumption turned out to be incorrect.

Playfair had been an assistant coach, but he had coached the defensemen, meaning we didn't have frequent contact. But he had treated me with enough respect that I didn't anticipate any difficulty playing for him. When I arrived after my stay at Hazelden, he sat me down and said he understood what I was going through. He told me his father had drinking issues. He assured me again that my status was the same as it was the previous season.

But I realized instantly that my place on Playfair's team was not the same place I held on Sutter's team. My status was different after I came back from rehab. Players treated me the same, but Playfair seemed to have a different attitude toward me.

Right or wrong, I just felt as if there was a wall up and I was on the outside looking in.

It is true that I wasn't in the best condition of my career because I couldn't skate while I was at Hazelden, but I wasn't embarrassingly out of shape. Plus, I'd always possessed the ability to get by while I was getting into shape, and the coaches knew that. At that point in my career, I was 34 years old and I had accepted the reality that I was going to be an eight- to 10-minute-per-game role player.

But Playfair was playing me five minutes per game, as if I had no value other than to fight. I quickly lost interest. It was unsettling for me to feel as if what I had to offer to a team wasn't appreciated.

Throughout my career, I was known as a loyal soldier. I would do anything for my team or any of my teammates. Loyalty is one of my strengths. When you treat me with respect, I'm all-in for you. But when I felt as if the coaches didn't appreciate my abilities, my emotions would sag. That's always been my Achilles heel. I need to feel some love coming from the coaches. I played like a commando every shift when I played for Scotty Bowman because I could feel that he appreciated what I could do, and cared about me as a person. I would have done anything for Darryl for the same reason.

But I didn't feel any connection with Playfair. Maybe that's my own insecurities talking. But that's how I felt.

I did talk to Darryl Sutter about my situation, but he said he had to allow Playfair to make his own decisions about players' playing time. Sutter is an honest man, and it was an honest answer. I expected that answer from him. He's not the kind of man that would tell his coach who to play. Sutter has a black-and-white, straightforward approach about what's right and what's wrong. In his mind, GMs manage, coaches coach, and players play. Even though he respected me, he was not going to disrupt the natural order of things. I respected him for that.

To make my situation worse, I developed a hernia issue that required surgery. I ended up playing 32 games, averaging just over five minutes per game.

That was the last season of my contract with the Flames, and I was looking forward to a fresh start elsewhere. But NHL Players Association officials called me to tell me they had other plans for me.

I had again tested positive for marijuana use. This was not a new occurrence. I frequently tested posited for marijuana use during my career. I'm guessing 30 or more times I tested positive for marijuana. But marijuana is not a performance enhancing drug, which meant the league couldn't suspend me for that alone.

The problem was that I had reached the point in my league-NHLPA mandated treatment phase that any substance abuse issues could prompt suspension.

Dan Cronin, director of the NHLPA substance abuse program, plus Dr. Brian Shaw and Dr. David Lewis, got me on a conference call and explained that I couldn't sign with another team. I would not be allowed to play again until I completed treatment and proved I could stay clean. They'd made arrangements for me to have a two-month expenses-paid trip to the Canyon Treatment Center in Malibu, California.

This wasn't a surprise to me. I knew the hammer was going to come down on me sooner or later, and I didn't fight it. Although I'm an addict, I have always known when it was time to listen to the people trying to help.

This was my fourth trip to a rehab center, and this was by far the best place I had been. If you are trying to overcome your addiction, it seems like trying to do it in plenty of sunshine makes some sense.

At the time I entered the program, Anna and I had planned to have a real wedding ceremony, and the treatment center counselors even agreed to let us go ahead with those plans.

I was allowed to go back to Calgary to renew our vows in August of 2007. I've been married three times, and had five ceremonies. I'm really good at it.

But I had plenty of time to think while I was at the treatment center. And in those two months it occurred to me that my marriage to Anna wasn't likely to work.

She wanted children, and I had been adamant with her that I didn't want any more children. That edict was difficult for Anna to accept. It was always going to be a source of friction between us.

When I returned to Calgary after my treatment, I told Anna I needed to return to Detroit to re-connect with my children. She wanted to go with me, but I said that I needed to go alone. I said I would send for her once I re-established my relationship with my children. She wanted me to stay in Calgary and work on our marriage. She told me that if I left, we were finished.

While she was at work, I wrote her a goodbye note, packed up my Chevy Avalanche truck with as many of belongings as would fit, and started the 32-hour drive to Detroit.

I loved Anna. She was a great wife. She loved me. She adored me. The truth is she probably loved and adored me too much. She is a beautiful person. I never meant to hurt her. She deserved better than I could give her.

I cannot tell you one story of her doing anything wrong or hurtful. She was just a victim of circumstance. At that time in my life, I didn't love myself so loving her was impossible. I was unfaithful to her. I had multiple affairs with ex-girlfriends and other random women on my trips to Michigan. She deserved much better than what I had to offer her at that time. She had conveniently been there for me at a time I was depressed. I never wanted to hurt her.

Although Anna initially accepted my demand that we would remain a childless couple, she eventually started to press the issue. Meanwhile, my ex-wife, Cheryl, had been pressuring me to return for the children's sake. If I stayed in Calgary I wasn't going to see my children much. That was certainly true. As I was trying to start a new life of sobriety, the pressure of dealing with Anna's understandable desire for a family and my family issues in Michigan became unbearable.

It was years before I realized how badly I treated Anna. I believe my ex-wife manipulated me through guilt.

Today, I do spend time thinking about what I need to do to be a good father. I felt like I left both Cheryl and the kids in good financial shape after the divorce, but I don't seem to get any credit for that. Although I was bankrupt, I made sure she and the kids were not. I made sure they were financially set so she would never have to get her first job ever, and so she could be home with the kids and still live very comfortably and lavishly. Even still though, today Cheryl has me battling in court over my pension and even recently went after me for child support. See, the problem I face now is that because of the money that I earned and gave to her she can afford the best and most expensive attorneys and I, on the other hand, can not. Ironic isn't it?

Now I can imagine what Anna thought when I told her I was going to live with my ex-wife for the sake of my children. Guilt is a beast as strong as alcohol when it comes to controlling me.

When I returned to Detroit, I actually moved into the basement of Cheryl's home. That wasn't a wise decision because it brought me back into the drama that I'd been trying to escape when I left Cheryl.

The problem was that my mother and sister stuck by Cheryl throughout our marital difficulty. If I didn't have some connection to Cheryl, then it was like I was ex-communicated. Because of their alliance with Cheryl, my family never really accepted my marriage to Anna. At that time of my life, it seemed important that I have the acceptance of my mother and sister.

My mother even flew to Minnesota to drive with me the rest of the way from Calgary.

The good news about Anna is that after I got out of her life she found the man she deserved to have. She finally had the baby she wanted, a boy named Declan. I've only talked to Anna twice since I left Calgary, but believe it or not, my current wife, Sheryl, has become friends with her. They started communicating because Anna realized that I had never signed divorce papers. They discovered they liked each other.

Sheryl tells me that Anna sounds content. That makes me ecstatic. She deserved to find the happiness I could not provide her.

I got out of rehab in September and I stayed in Calgary into November. When I started my trip back to Detroit, I already had a plan in my head about what I wanted to do next: I wanted to resume my NHL career.

While I was in rehab, I had been eating healthy and my weight was good. It's funny what you remember. We were served ostrich for dinner one night at the Malibu treatment center. It was actually quite good.

When I was in rehab, I also befriended a Nigerian soccer player and he and I worked out together. I believed I could still play.

But I needed help to get back in the game. There were many people I could have called to help me, but there was only one I wanted to call. It was Kris Draper. I'd always had his back on the ice, and he always tried to have my back off the ice, even though I wasn't always willing to accept his help.

I called him and asked him to meet me for lunch. We sat at the table, reminisced, and then I put it to him bluntly: "I need your help."

"Whatever you need," he said.

The only advice he gave me was to get rid of my red-tinted Mohawk haircut and not to wear my Grinder hat.

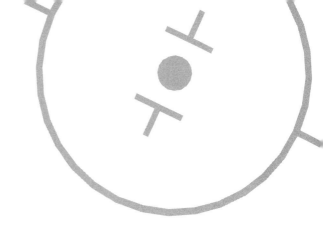

Chapter 12

2008

*"Knock me down, gonna get back up, thought
you seen the last of me but I ain't had enough,
come to town gonna get what's mine … I'm
a Detroit son of a bitch, no way you can fuck
with this, got one chance left Im'a take it"*

—"Detroit Son of a Bitch"
Dirty Americans

2008

When you travel through life at 100 mph, you miss all the scenery. The first 15 years of my pro hockey career were a blur.

I was so busy being a player and sampling its rewards that I never enjoyed the ride. When Detroit general manager Ken Holland and his assistant Jim Nill told me after Thanksgiving in 2007 that they would consider re-signing me if I could prove I still had what it takes, it felt like I was getting a mulligan. At age 35, I was going to be back in the minor leagues, playing for $500 per week, for the Flint (Michigan) Generals of the International Hockey League.

I couldn't have been happier.

After a divorce, a bankruptcy, the death of James Anders, and four trips to rehabilitation for substance abuse, I had re-discovered the joy of playing hockey. Sober and clear-headed, I'd been working out at Draper's Core Training Facility in Troy. Dr. Jeff Pierce supervised my training, and I made it clear that I was ready to do whatever it was going to require for me to return to the NHL.

I didn't miss any training sessions, and even Draper remarked on how committed I was to this comeback. He seemed impressed with my focus. This was not a half-assed effort on my part. This was a man who finally remembered how much he enjoyed playing hockey.

Holland didn't promise me anything, but he didn't need to. We had known each other for many years. When he said he would seriously consider signing me, I knew he meant it.

My friendship with Draper had lost its energy after I left Detroit. We would text, but I kept him at arm's length. Honestly, I avoided contact with him when I was drinking because I didn't want him to be disappointed in me. I knew he would call me out on my drinking. It meant a great deal to me that he was willing to go to Holland and vouch for the seriousness of my intent to return to the NHL.

Also, I wanted to re-ignite my friendship with him because I need well-grounded people like Draper in my life. He was like a brother to me for so many years.

Draper was a part-owner of the Flint Generals, and he suggested I start my comeback there. I also knew another Generals owner, Ron Sanko, who was the team's director of hockey operations. My favorite rock 'n' roll bar, the Machine Shop, is in Flint. The great Michigan State guard Mateen Cleaves was from Flint. I was as stoked to go to Flint as LeBron James was to go to South Beach. I am serious when I say that. I was mentally invested into this comeback.

When I went to Flint, I was looking to accomplish two objectives—to get down to my ideal playing weight and to regain some confidence. Bothered by a sports hernia, I didn't score a single goal in my 32 games with Calgary in 2006–07. I simply hadn't played much in the past 18 months.

The Flint coach was Kevin Kerr, and I knew about him because he had played for the Windsor Spitfires from 1984 to 1987. I was four years younger and I remember watching Kerr terrorize opponents with his physical abilities and his hands in the Ontario Hockey League. He could score 20 goals and he could hammer guys. He amassed more than 700 penalty minutes in three seasons with the Spits.

Kerr registered 352 penalty minutes in his first pro season for Rochester in the AHL in 1987–88. He never made the NHL, but his legacy included a long list of victims in the minor leagues. He was my kind of coach. I knew we would get along.

I ended up playing 11 games for the Generals, and Kerr did me a great favor by giving me the ice time I needed to regain a strong conditioning level. In fact, I had more ice time per game than I'd had in my last three seasons in the NHL. It didn't take me long to shed the extra pounds and to improve my conditioning.

To say I enjoyed my time in Flint would be an understatement. The team had a good mix of youngsters and veteran minor leaguers.

It had been 16 years since I had ridden a bus on a hockey road trip. But even that seemed like fun to me. The Generals' bus was nicknamed "Cessie," short for Cesspool. You can draw your own conclusions as to why we called it that. But this bus looked like it had been driven straight to Flint from the movie *Slap Shot.*

Sometimes the heat worked, sometimes it didn't. But honestly, the guys didn't mind too much because the bus rides were usually a comedy show. My three weeks in Flint were probably the best time I had playing hockey since the season the Red Wings won the Stanley Cup in 2002.

I ended up playing on a line with Jason Cirone, a player my age who I had played against in the Ontario Hockey League. He played for the Cornwall Royals back then, and then he went on to have a memorable career in Europe. He even established himself enough as an Italian to play for that country at the Olympics.

We were both living in the suburbs north of Detroit, and on practice days Jason would pick me up and then we would meet forwards John DiPace and Mike Kinnie at the Great Lakes Crossing shopping center in Auburn Hills, Michigan. The four of us would commute together, with me riding shotgun. I spent the entire trip busting balls and scheming about who we might prank that day.

Playing with Cirone was fun because he could thread a needle with his passes. In Flint, I felt as if I had an offensive role. It was fun to play a ton of minutes and play those minutes believing my shifts were important to the outcome of the game.

In my last season in Calgary, I lost interest because it seemed as if coach Jim Playfair didn't respect what I had to offer. It's difficult to feel essential to the team's success when you're only playing four or five minutes per game.

When I agreed to play in the IHL, one of the thoughts was that the IHL tough guys were going to want to measure themselves against a proven NHL enforcer. But that never happened. In fact, the opposite occurred, as opponents mostly didn't bother me out of respect for what I had accomplished in the NHL.

The only moment of disrespect directed toward me came in my last game with the Generals on January 27, 2008. The Red Wings had seen enough to ask me to go Grand Rapids in the American Hockey League to continue my preparation to return to the NHL.

We were playing against the Kalamazoo Wings, and at the end of the second period I came out to the point to cover the defenseman, at which time Kalamazoo player Travis Granbois took a two-hander across my pants.

I remember thinking that I should skate away because this was my last game in Flint. But Granbois was the Sean Avery of the IHL. And he had been acting like an asshole. He needed his ass kicked.

Couldn't skate away.

"You motherfucker," I screamed. "You're gonna regret that slash."

I grabbed his chin strap, and twisted it until he felt like he was choking.

Obviously, everyone in the hockey world know how much anger I brought to my Claude Lemieux battle. The only other NHL guy I can remember wanting to hurt badly was Jamal Mayers. He was respected around the NHL as a guy who played hard, but Mayers raised my anger by jumping me once and I was always looking for the opportunity to make him pay for that.

I will admit here that I wanted to hurt Granbois as badly as I wanted to hurt Lemieux and Mayers.

"You little bitch," I screamed at Granbois. "You think you want to try to go big time on me?"

His face was turning beet red.

"So how do you like playing big-boy hockey?" I asked him as I kept twisting his chin strap.

He was on the bottom of the pile, and his feet were kicking when the linesman stepped in and saved him further embarrassment.

Even though it was my last game in the IHL, I wasn't going to let Granbois get away with that shit.

Although I can't be sure, Granbois may have momentarily passed out because he was having trouble breathing.

"So you think you're so fucking smart now?" I asked him. "Well this is how we played the game back in the day. And trust me, you wouldn't be able to cut it."

I was 13 years older than this punk Granbois. When he was eight, I was fighting guys like Joey Kocur, Donald Brashear, Kelly Buchberger, and Derian Hatcher. I was not going to let him get away with a cheap shot against me.

The trick of putting your fingers through the ear hole and twisting the strap is an old-school move. When you do that and put an opponent in a headlock, he will panic in a hurry.

I didn't hit him. I think I tried to gouge his eyes out. I didn't give a fuck. He pissed me off because he tried to make a name for himself. When he was flopping around on the ice like a fish, I told him, "You don't have what it takes, kid."

The only other fight I had in the IHL involved Muskegon tough-guy Chris Kovalcik, who might be the most respectful enforcer I ever met.

We lined up for a faceoff, and Kovalcik said to me, "You're my idol and it would be an honor to fight you. Would you fight me?"

I didn't want to fight him, but how could I refuse that respectful challenge? So I dropped the gloves, and I kind of swatted away his punches, and we wrestled around. It wasn't much of a fight.

But the kid said something like, "This has been the best day of my life."

It was my honor just to meet him. What a respectful athlete. But that's not the whole story.

Holland heard that I had a fight with the Muskegon tough guy and that I didn't aggressively pound him.

When I got to Grand Rapids, Holland came up to me and said, "You don't want to fight anymore? You let an IHL heavyweight manhandle you. Do you still have it?"

Holland loved razzing me about one thing or another.

"Are you kidding me?" I said. "I didn't want to hurt the kid. I could have killed him. After the game, I think I signed an autograph for him."

When you factor in my experience with the Grand Rapid Griffins and then my return to Detroit, I think I had as much fun playing hockey in 2007–08 as I had ever had.

In my Griffins debut, on February 15, 2008, I scored three goals and added one assist in a 6–3 win against the Lake Erie Monsters.

It was $1 hot dog night at Van Andel Arena, and some fans threw hot dogs as well as hats after I scored my third goal at 2:45 of the third period, a booming slap shot past Lake Erie goalie Mike Wall's blocker.

One fan even threw a shoe on the ice to celebrate the hat trick. I have no idea what that was about.

The announced crowd of 10,062 gave me a four-minute standing ovation. It was quite a night. It was the largest crowd the Griffins had drawn since opening night. According to MLive.com, the team had a walk-up sale of about 1,700 tickets in the last few hours before game time.

"What can you say, this is like a movie script," Griffins coach Mike Stothers told the media.

Darren Helm assisted on my first goal at 5:53 of the first period. Wall had stopped his shot but surrendered a juicy rebound, and I drove it home quickly, just like Brendan Shanahan had taught me to do years before.

My second goal came on the power play. I stuffed a backhand wrap-around past Wall in the second period.

I told the media that the game showed me that "I am doing the right things" that would put me on the path to returning to the NHL.

I truly believed that I could step in and help the Red Wings in 2007–08 the way Joey Kocur stepped in and helped the Red Wings when Holland signed him out of the beer league in 1996–97.

One of the best aspects of my time spent with the Griffins was the fact that my son Griffin was 11 and old enough to enjoy being around a pro team.

Stothers allowed him to announce the lineup before the game and he even took a road trip to Peoria with us.

The Griffins were formed in 1996, the same year that Griffin was born. And he got into his head that the Griffins were named in his honor.

Stothers was an old-school coach, and those are my favorite kind of coaches. He would tear a strip off you if you weren't playing well, and I have never minded that because I feel like you know where you stand with old-school coaches.

He was tough to the point that his tirades could be downright funny. We were down 1–0 after two periods against Rochester, and he came into the dressing room and emptied both chambers on all of us. It reminded me of the way Mavety used to fire away at us in my junior days. No one was spared his wrath that night.

Garrett Stafford got pummeled, and all of the top players were singled out. Then he walked across to forward Tyler Redenbach, a former Western Hockey League standout who wore his very white hair in an afro.

"And you, Q-Tip, when are you going to start showing some jam?" Stothers bellowed.

I buried my head in my towel to prevent Stothers from knowing that I was laughing my ass off. I peeked out and caught team captain Mark Hartigan doing the same thing. It may have been the funniest coach yelling episode I've ever heard.

Playing for Stothers in Grand Rapids made hockey fun again. It's said that old-timers don't have anything in common with younger minor leaguers, but I had a blast.

One reason why I'm still very interested in the Red Wings' success today is that I feel like players such as Jimmy Howard, Jonathan Ericsson, Darren Helm, Justin Abdelkader, Kyle Quincey, and Joakim Andersson are my guys.

I feel connected to them, and I hope they feel like I helped them in some way when we played together in Grand Rapids. Maybe I couldn't show them how to score like Brendan Shanahan showed me, but I felt like I schooled them in some of the tricks of the trade, like how to protect yourself in the corners or how to defend yourself in a fight.

I feel like I have watched Jimmy Howard grow up in the Detroit organization.

Ten days after I netted a hat trick for Grand Rapids, Holland had seen enough to sign me to a $600,000 pro-rated contract. I had been playing in Grand Rapids for $75,000, pro-rated, meaning I was making about $2,800 per week before taxes. But at that point in my life, I probably would have played for free just for the opportunity to get back to the show.

Even after I signed, I had to spend two more weeks in Grand Rapids on a conditioning stint.

The truth is that Red Wings coach Mike Babcock was not as convinced as Holland was that I could help the team.

But when I played my first game back with the Red Wings on March 28, 2008, Babcock started the Grind Line. I was out there playing with Draper and Kirk Maltby. It was a classy gesture by Babcock.

I ended up only playing three regular season games, but I believe I played well enough in the season finale against Chicago to earn a place in the playoff lineup. I seemed to win the 12th forward role over Aaron Downey.

Per my tradition, I did score an important playoff goal, netting the team's first goal in a 4–2 win against the Nashville Predators. It wasn't the biggest goal of my career, but it sure felt that way at the time, given the climb I'd made to get back to the NHL.

"You can't help but cheer for people who are trying to get their life back on track, especially when a guy has worked as hard as he has and has been one of the favorite sons here in Detroit," Babcock told the media after the game.

Babcock is not a players coach. He can be infuriating. That's why I appreciated his comments after that game.

Johan Franzen and Tomas Holmstrom both had injuries, and I was able to stay in the lineup for 17 playoff games. I didn't lose my spot until the Stanley Cup Final, when the injured players were all back.

But when we celebrated the Stanley Cup championship on Pittsburgh's home ice, I was just as thrilled as I was when I won my other three titles. I felt like I had done enough during the playoffs to share in the success of this Stanley Cup.

Draper said the fact that I was able to lift the Stanley Cup again was "a Disney script."

In one respect, the fourth Cup was the best Cup for family purposes. My four children—Griffin, Emerson, Avery, and Gracyn—were all old enough to appreciate celebrating the championship with their dad. At the time, Griffin, my oldest, was 12 and Gracyn was four.

Our day with the Stanley Cup included a stop at Stroh's Ice Cream Parlor, where we filled up Lord Stanley's mug with chocolate, vanilla, strawberry, and cookie dough ice cream, plus chocolate syrup and sprinkle toppings.

We took the Stanley Cup to the Greek Islands Coney Island for breakfast, and then the barber shop, St. Regis Catholic School, and the Core Training Facility in Troy where Jeff Pierce and his staff helped me start my comeback.

It was the perfect day for a sober man who thought he had turned around his life. On that day, spent with my family in celebration of my hockey career, I felt like I had my life back under control. But I was wrong, as I had been many times before.

Chapter 13

Follow the Money

"It's okay for you to hate me, for all the things I've done, I've made a few mistakes, but I'm not the only one ... You pulled me under, to save yourself"

—"Coming Down"
Five Finger Death Punch

Follow the Money

When I played in the National Hockey League, every day was Christmas, and I was Santa Claus. I earned more than $16 million during my 15-season career and I tried to take care of everybody in the world with that money.

One of the misconceptions about my career was that I went broke because of drugs and gambling.

The truth is that I lost my wealth because I couldn't say no to anyone who had his or her hand out. I was the fucking Bank of McCarty. I was Daddy Warbucks. It seemed as if anyone who needed a "loan" to survive during difficult times came to me.

About 10 years ago, one of my closest friends found himself in a financial mess because his investments went south. I loaned him $100,000 to dig himself out of the hole he was in. I gave it to him because we were tight. We were like family. There was a time when I golfed with the man almost every day. I was a godfather to one of his children. I never hesitated to give him that loan.

He made one $10,000 payment to me. As of this writing, I haven't seen or heard from that friend in more than seven years.

Another time, a former member of the Detroit Red Wings organization—not a player—needed a financial boost to help a distressed business venture, so I loaned him $50,000. I have never received a dime of that money back. If I saw him today, I would probably punch him right in the fucking mouth.

You're probably wondering why I won't name him, but that's just not how I operate. I can't throw him under the bus. It's not in me. When I have a beef with someone, it's about me and him. I'm not going to embarrass him publicly, even though my dirty laundry is always on public display.

My estimate is that I gave away about $1 million to friends, family members, and acquaintances during my NHL career. My gambling losses, and the amount of money I spent on drugs, wouldn't total anywhere near that amount of money.

Today, I'm living on an NHL pension of $636 per month and whatever I can earn for autograph or promotional appearances. Now that I'm living month-to-month, like everyone else, it's funny how I don't have as many friends as I used to have.

I'm not telling you this to earn your pity. I'm offering this truth only because I'm hoping that some young NHL prospect might read this chapter and avoid the same mistakes that I made by not managing my earnings with my future in mind.

My money woes are my own fault. When you grow up without having money, and then you earn big money, it isn't always easy to know how to handle it. I always spent money as if I had an endless supply.

I didn't start out as a free spender. My first NHL contract paid me $200,000 per season, with a $200,000 signing bonus. After taxes, I cleared about $140,000, and I remember my stepdad made me put $100,000 in the bank.

My first major purchase was a 1991 Jeep Cherokee with the extended cab. I bought some golf clubs, and gave some money to Mom and Dad and Cheryl's parents. Cheryl's engagement ring came out of the money as well.

Looking back, I wonder now why I gave $10,000 to my girlfriend's parents. That was just the start of me being overly generous with my money.

Would they have given me $10,000 if they won the lottery? I know it's proper to give your parents a home or a car or a major gift out of your signing bonus, but how many stories have you read about athletes signing their first contracts and giving their girlfriend's parents money? I don't think I've read any stories like that.

I tell this story only to point out that I was overly generous. My advice to an athlete today would be to invest the bulk of their money from their first contact.

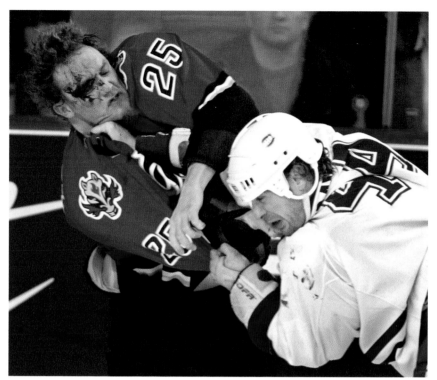

With the Calgray Flames, here I am fighting with Sheldon Souray of the Canadiens. (AP Images)

Performing with Grinder (Getty Images)

Ozzie, Malts, me, and Drapes in front of Lenin's tomb in Red Square, Moscow.

Eating ice cream out of the 2008 Stanley Cup.

Holding up the Cup with my mom and my sister.

Griffin and me hanging out with the '08 Cup.

Anna Okuszko and I on the day we had an actual post–Las Vegas wedding in Calgary, Alberta.

Here I am as an analyst on Versus in 2011, doing what I love to do—talking hockey.

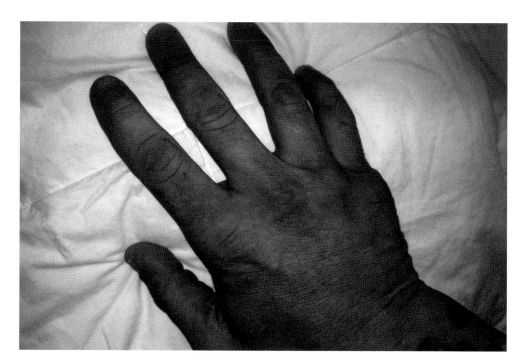

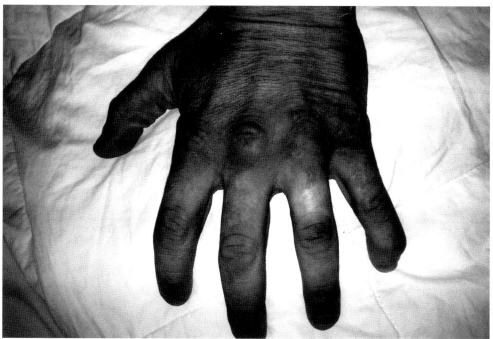

The hands of a fighter today. Ouch!

Reuniting with my Black Label Society brothers in 2011 at Joe Louis Arena after hanging with Zakk Wylde on the tour bus.

With X-Pac (Sean Waltman) in my backyard on Clearwater Beach.

The past rears its ugly head. Front page of the Detroit News *and many other news outlets in Michigan, unfortunately.*

Sheryl and me. As her brothers tell me, my wife is the best shot in her family. When I look at this picture I can hear her saying her favorite quote: "You can think it's a game if you want to."

Sheryl and me. This is one of my favorite pictures—I'm right where I want to be.

Considering that just having that amount of money made me feel like a big roller, imagine how I felt when I signed my first big contract of $4.5 million over five years. And I was just getting started. As a player, you get paid twice a month, and I remember that one of my goals was to reach the point where my take-home pay was more than $100,000 per paycheck. That finally happened in 2002–03, when my annual salary was $2.2 million.

My take-home that season was about $102,000 per paycheck. I remember being fucking giddy that I had finally reached six figures.

Of course that made me wonder what kind of money Nick Lidstrom and Stevie Y were bringing down twice a month. Once, on payday, I remember going up to Nick and saying, "Nick, I gotta see your check. C'mon, I just have to see what that looks like."

Lidstrom is such a nice guy that he showed me. It was around $425,000 or something near that. It was a stupid amount of money. But what I was earning seemed more stupid. If anyone deserved to make that amount of money, it was Nick.

When it came to money, I didn't know how to be conservative. Instead of planning ahead like my teammates Kris Draper and Kirk Maltby did, I lived for the fucking moment because that is my personality.

I like to spread around my money. I often tipped 50 percent, which is why they always rolled out the red carpet for me everywhere I went in Detroit. I took care of people wherever I went.

I made plenty of impulsive, frivolous purchases during my career, like the time I gave Chris Chelios $10,000 for his black 1965 Mustang convertible.

As it turned out, the sweet Mustang was one of the few investments that actually paid off for me. I needed work done on my home, and I gave that Mustang to a contractor who knocked $12,000 off my bill.

But did I need that Mustang? Of course not. I didn't need most of the shit I bought during my career. I spent money mostly because I had money.

During my NHL career, I probably drove every style of SUV that was being manufactured.

When I attended charity auctions, I'd spend $5,000 on items just because I could. At a Detroit Country Day School auction, I once spent $5,000 on a golf cart. I used that golf cart to drive my kids around the neighborhood.

I paid for my sister to go to college. I allowed my wife and mother to buy what they needed. I liked sharing my wealth. I'm only half-joking when I say that other people spent more of my money than I did.

When I filed for bankruptcy in 2006, people assumed that it was tied to a gambling or drug addiction. People actually have said to me, "Did you put your money up your nose?"

People just assume I had a cocaine problem, and that is not what happened.

If you review the court documents of my bankruptcy, my money woes are explained in verifiable detail.

There were four reasons why I owed more money than I had. First, the 2004–05 NHL season was canceled because of a lockout, and I lost about $2 million in wages.

Plus, I lost money in an ill-advised land deal, made bad loans to friends totaling $490,000, and got divorced from Cheryl.

When the Red Wings bought out my contract in 2006, I was scheduled to make $1.7 million, but they only had to give me two-thirds, and the government got its share for taxes. Then 75 percent of that payout had to go to my wife because of our divorce settlement.

The accounting of my bankruptcy shows that I owed $6.2 million in 2006 and I had assets totaling $1.9 million. But my asset total was misleading because one of my listed assets was my Farmington Hills house that was worth less than I owed on it. And my assets included the non-secured loans I had made to friends that were never going to be repaid.

My gambling debt totaled $185,000: I owed $100,000 to the Bellagio Casino in Las Vegas, $60,000 to the Palms Casino in Las Vegas, and $25,000 to the MotorCity Casino in Detroit.

What I owed to casinos may seem outrageous to you, but it could have been far worse. At the height of my playing career, my lines of credit at Las Vegas casinos probably totaled about $800,000. That's how much money they would have given me to gamble just by me signing my name.

I had lines of credit between $100,000 and $200,000 at most of the casinos. My worst problem was not my own gambling, but my willingness to allow my friends to use my lines of credit. As previously mentioned, I wasn't as wild in my gambling as I was in my substance abuse. I never gambled all that I had, and I usually knew when to quit. The same can't be said about my drinking and drug use.

But when I would go to Las Vegas I would usually be with others—particularly one man who I viewed as a trusted business partner. I would often let him use my line, and he would gamble heavily.

He had the craziest run of gambling success I ever saw one night at the Desert Inn in Las Vegas. He tapped into one of my credit lines, sat down at a craps table, and won $428,000. He paid back the credit line, and gave me $25,000 for my troubles. As I recall, he gave the casino employee a $35,000 tip.

The general idea of craps is simple: a shooter rolls the dice and if he gets a seven or 11 on his first roll he wins. If he throws a two, three, or 12, then he craps out, meaning he loses his bet. If the shooter throws any other number, he or she must then roll that number again before throwing a seven. If the seven comes up before the point is made, the bets are lost.

That night my so-called partner made 15 successful passes to earn almost half a million dollars.

The funny part of the story is that he was slamming down two Captain Morgan and Cokes for every pass he made. You can do the math. By the end of his run of luck, he was barely standing.

He had to hold on to the table just to stay upright.

Just before his last roll, I yelled, "Bring it home, big guy!"

"Hell," he said, "I can't even see the end of the table."

Some of us moved in to steady him as he made his final successful throw.

When he was done with that roll, it was clearly time for him to retire. As the muscle in the group, I had to be the one to take charge of carrying him out of there. This was also a time when I was not drinking, meaning I was in the best position to complete the mission. It was a formidable task because he probably weighed 260 pounds at the time.

But I threw him over my shoulder and started marching him to his room, which seemed like it was located half a mile away. It was on the opposite end of the casino.

Some of our other buddies helped me throw him onto his bed. We just threw his chip winnings in the bed with him. When he woke, he found all of these $25,000 chips and had no idea how he'd managed to accumulate so many.

Looking back, I was fortunate that my association with this guy didn't get me into even more trouble than it did. Sometimes he would use my lines of credit as a short-term business loan because you have 30 interest-free days. We would use the credit line, do some gambling for appearance sake, and then cash in a few chips here and there so he could make a payment he needed to make.

It was not a smart move by me, but he always managed to pay the loans back…until the very end.

However, this is the same guy who convinced me to enter into a business deal that was at the heart of my financial collapse. More than $650,000 of my debt was for a land-purchase deal in Hartland, Michigan, that went sour. I was a partner in the purchase of 28 acres of land near M-59. The idea was that my partner was going to develop the land and we were going to make a killing. But the land was never developed.

As in most of my business relationships, I was too trusting. I always took people at their word. If you told me that you were going to pay me back, I believed you.

As part of the land deal, we owned a gas station on the property. We were supposed to use the profit from that to pay down our debt on the land.

When my land deal wasn't working the way my partner said it would, I did question the lack of progress in developing the property. He assured me that it was all going according to plan. I accepted his word, even though other friends warned me not to trust him.

My loss on that property was about $250,000 in cash, a large sum of money, considering that my earning ability had started to decline by then.

Since that land deal went bankrupt, I have only seen my former partner one time. I was at the Chris Chelios–owned restaurant near Comerica Park on the opening day of the baseball season a few years ago, and he was coming up the stairs as I was going down.

He fled out the back door before we had a chance to "talk."

Of all of my issues, gambling probably caused the least amount of trouble for me because I didn't take it lightly when I lost money.

One of my favorite gambling stories is a fun tale involving Kris Draper. It's fun for me because Draper is one of the least likely people to be anywhere near a casino. The story begins at Draper's bachelor's party, which started in Michigan and ended up in Las Vegas.

It was the summer of 1999, and I was Draper's best man. It was a great day of golf and drinking, and we ended up at Chris Osgood's home in Birmingham, where the party raged until 4:30 AM, when I had to gather up Drapes for a planned morning flight to Los Angeles. He and I had to film a PlayStation commercial out there and filming began around 10:00 AM, Pacific time.

At that point in my life I wasn't drinking, so it was my job to look after those who were. As you would expect when dealing with a bachelor party, Drapes was in rough shape. But I folded him into the car, tucked him into his first-class seat, got him an orange, and he was good to go. Of course, flight attendants had to wake us when we landed in L.A.

Filming went smoothly and we were finished at 3:30 in the afternoon, but our return flight to Detroit wasn't until 7:00 PM the next day. Drapes wanted to go to bed. I wanted to go to Vegas. Guess who won that argument? Draper had never been to Las Vegas, and his best man couldn't allow him to get married without having been to Sin City.

I called a buddy at the Desert Inn Casino and he had us hooked up with plane tickets and a suite within minutes. We were in Las Vegas by 6:00 PM. Of course, Draper was sound asleep, face-first in his bed, by 6:15. I went to the casino by myself, lost a couple of grand, and had an early night by my standards.

The next morning, Draper was fully functional again and both of us were starving. I don't think Draper had eaten anything the day before. We essentially ordered every item on the left side of the room service breakfast menu. We had several trays of food. Our room looked like an all-you-can-eat buffet.

By 10:00 AM I was ready to gamble again. The problem is that Drapes doesn't like to gamble. He likes to hide his money in his mattress. But I convinced him to come and play with my money. At that point in my life, baccarat was my game of choice. I got a $5,000 marker, sat Draper down at the game, explained the rules, showed him how to roll the cards, and several hours later we got up with stacks and stacks of chips.

When we started, Drapes had no idea how to play the game, but when our day was done we cashed in more than $90,000 in chips. At one point, Draper won 17 consecutive hands. I gave him $10,000 for his work, and walked around the airport with more than $80,000 in cash.

Coincidentally, the table at the Desert Inn was the same table where former teammate Kevin Hodson had sat 12 hours with me while I played during the 1999 All-Star break. Hodson was one of the funniest teammates I ever had, and he had everyone cracking up with his cheering and dancing during my baccarat session.

My biggest loss at a casino was $175,000 in about 12 hours of playing blackjack. That includes losing $40,000 on one hand. At one point, I was actually leaving to go to the airport with $64,000 in my possession, but I decided to stop and play a few more hands before I left.

I placed a bet of $8,000 and drew two eights. I split eights, and drew a two and another eight. So I split that eight. And then I drew the fourth eight. Now I had five bets of $8,000 in from of me. I had some good hands, including a 20, two 18s, and a 17. The dealer had a six showing, and then turned over a face card. Then he caught a five and my $40,000 became the casino's $40,000. That night in 2003 was the last time I ever played high-stakes blackjack.

Since then, I've confined my gambling to the occasional slot machines. To be honest, I like to see numbers spin because it stimulates my ADHD.

But now I take $100 and play with that for three or four hours. I'm no longer trying to break the bank.

In my sports-betting heyday, I would bet between $1,000 and $5,000 on a game. The last time I bet on sports I lost $60,000 on my collection of bets. I quit sports betting that night.

In about 2003, I started playing poker seriously, mostly at the old MotorCity Casino. I was in some big games. I played in some games with pro players such as Scotty Nguyen and Erik Seidel. Probably because of my ADD, my brain seems to function a bit differently than a normal brain and I have a good success rate at reading hands on the board.

I never went real crazy in my poker playing, but I always enjoyed playing the game. The biggest pot I ever won was $47,000, and that came in an Omaha game at the Bellagio against World Series of Poker–champion Josh Arieh and pro Terry Fleischer.

Holding a five, six, seven, eight, and being two suited, I went all in for $17,000.

The flop was a three, four, and a King. The pro players weren't concerned about me. They went after each other and their side pot was worth more than $100,000.

I won the hand with the straight, but Arieh won his match with a pair of aces against a pair of queens.

It didn't always go that well for me. I remember being in a game against World Series of Poker–champion Antonio "the Magician" Esfandiari and going all in with a pair of fours in the hole and a four on the flop and getting beat by three nines.

The bankruptcy was an embarrassing situation because my financial mess became public record. Newspapers even wrote about 300 people showing up to buy my personal shit. One of the auction managers told reporters that usually 50 to 100 people show up for a bankruptcy action, but the lure of buying an athlete's belongings tripled the crowd.

I was already in Calgary playing for the Flames when the auction took place, but I was told one dude showed up wearing a McCarty No. 25 Red Wings jersey.

Somebody paid $175 for my bath mats and coffee maker. I don't believe I paid that much for those items when I bought them new. It didn't seem like anyone got any bargains. A collection of my pots, pans, toaster, mixer, and towels went for $240. My Buddha statue went for $450.

I'd never really been a heavy memorabilia collector, so I didn't lose too many items of sentimental value. I did lose my collection of *South Park* memorabilia, most of it autographed by creators Matt Stone and Trey Parker.

In terms of sentimental value, the big losses were two motorcycles, including my chrome-plated Harley-Davidson. That was the bike I rode when I was cruising with Bob Probert and Vinnie Johnson and the boys. Many fine hours were logged on that Harley.

One bike was sold as a package with my leather jacket and helmet. That helmet had a sticker on it that read: "Ass, grass, or gas—no one rides for free."

Kind of sums up my life, doesn't it?

My favorite bike and gear sold for $9,300. The footnote of that story is that a few years later the man who bought the jacket met me and gave it back to me as a gift. That was after my retirement, meaning I'm a bit hazy on the details. It was a random act of kindness. But I was thankful to get the jacket back because I wore that jacket during my glory years with the Red Wings.

The items I'm glad didn't end up in the hands of strangers were my Stanley Cup championship rings from 1997, 1998, and 2002. My ex-wife, Cheryl, made a deal with the creditors to buy the rings so my children could have them. They are tucked safely away in a safe deposit box.

The only championship ring I still own is the 2008 ring, which obviously came after my bankruptcy.

When I look back now, I see that I never had as much money as I thought I did. Even when you are making a million per year, the tendency is to try to live better than you should be. When I made a million dollars, the taxes ate up about 37 percent and my agent took 3 percent. I bought more house than I needed, and spent more on vehicles than I should have. When I started to earn that much, I was also paying off the debt I occurred before I was making that much.

It didn't help that, as I mentioned earlier, I spent well over $400,000 out of my own pocket to keep Grinder on stage through the years. When we did have paid gigs, some of the profit went to the charitable foundation that bears my father's name.

Everyone believes that if they came into money they would be smart about how they spend it. But all you have to do as look at the history of lottery winners to know that earning big money doesn't mean you will automatically be smart about spending money.

If you are earning $100,000 per paycheck, it can go just as quickly as if you are earning hundreds of dollars.

Never did I have a chance to recover financially after my bankruptcy. I was 33 when I filed, and I was upfront with the Flames about my financial difficulties when I signed with them in 2006.

In my two seasons in Calgary, I earned $800,000 per season. But under the terms of the Settlement Agreement for my divorce, I agreed to give my ex-wife 75 percent of all of my income starting at the time of the divorce (in February 2005) until I retired from the NHL in 2009. I agreed to give her all the money in every bank account that we had before the bankruptcy was filed, plus the house, which we purchased at over $1.3 million. When you subtract the amount of money I paid in taxes and then paid to my ex-wife, there wasn't much left to live on, let alone to plan for the future.

I don't remember exactly how much money I had in the bank right after I retired, but I'm guessing it was around $5,000. When you count some insurance policies I had, my net worth was probably roughly $50,000. But I still had family obligations and I needed to live, and that money evaporated quickly.

I was an analyst for Versus for about 18 months, and television paid reasonably well and kept me afloat, but when NBC took over Versus, my boss lost his job. That meant that the people he hired were also gone. Since then, I've worked briefly in radio and at a pawn shop. But neither job paid all that well.

As I write this book, I have no income I can count on except my pension and my wife's RN income, but amazingly I am happier now than I ever was as a millionaire.

That's the story of my financial demise. If you were expecting to hear a tale of me losing millions of dollars at the blackjack table or having huge debts with a drug dealer, you are probably disappointed.

I liked to gamble, but I was never a runaway train when it came to losing money. If I lost too much, I could walk away. I never bet on hockey. It was mostly on football games.

When it came to drugs, my drug of choice was weed, and that's an affordable habit. Plus, I had friends everywhere who gave me weed for free. I didn't need to carry a stash with me because I always had friends who would have it on them. I never even would've considered trying to cross the border with pot on me. I'm an addict, but I've maintained enough control to be smart about my addiction.

My financial rise and fall has given me a different perspective than I had at the height of my career. When I was in the prime of my career with the Red Wings, I had a home in West Bloomfield, Michigan, that had about 5,000 square feet, plus a finished basement that covered 2,500 square feet.

Today, I live in 1,400 square feet, and I wonder why the hell I needed all of that space back then.

If I could talk to a player receiving his first NHL contract, my advice would be not to spend your money as if you will be earning that amount of money the rest of your life. Don't buy more than you need. Buy a nice ride, and live well, but don't buy a 5,000-foot house when you only need 1,400 square feet.

And above all else, don't let other people spend your fucking money. Learn to say no.

"Easy for you to say, your heart has never been broken, your pride has never been stolen, not yet, not yet"

—"These Days"
Foo Fighters

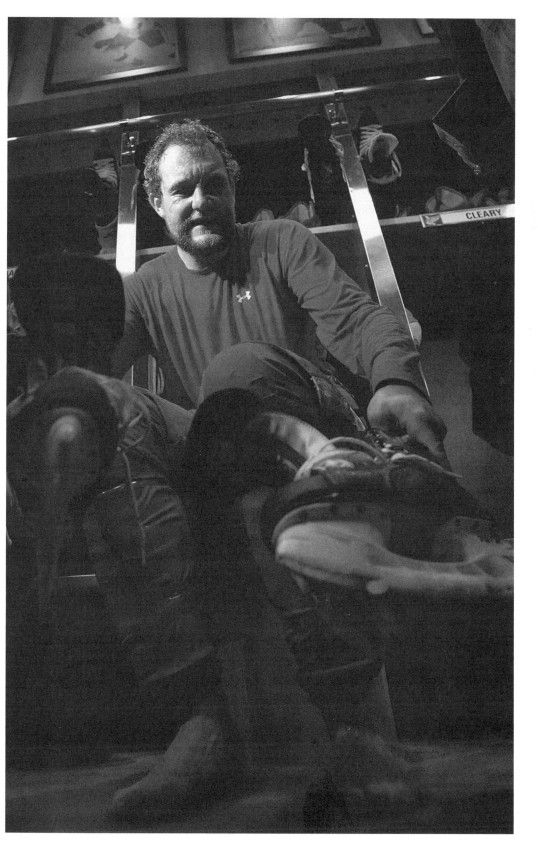

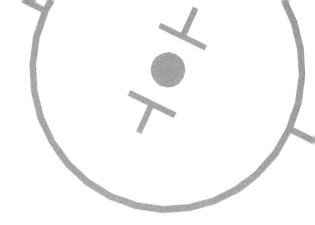

Chapter 14

Reflections

"I've been cut, I've been opened up, I've been shattered by the ones I thought I loved, you left me here like a chalk outline, on the sidewalk, waiting for the rain, to wash away"

—"Chalk Outline"
Three Days Grace

Reflections

You will never hear me blame the hockey culture for my substance abuse issues.

Never will I say that I drank because I had to fight. My addiction is a complicated matter that involves every aspect of my life and my personality.

In 1996, when I admitted I needed help to deal with my problem, my stepfather, Craig, was already battling multiple myeloma. I remember he told me, "We both suffer from a disease. Let's just lean on each other for support and maybe we can help each other get through it."

It was probably the first time that I ever considered that I was dealing with a disease. It didn't matter whether I was a fireman, a lawyer, or a hockey player. I have wires crossed somewhere that makes my response to alcohol different than people's. It didn't matter what profession I chose.

Still, based on what we've seen happen over the last few years in the NHL, you have to wonder if you are doing long-term damage to your health when you play the role of an NHL tough guy.

The deaths of NHL tough-guys Derek Boogaard, Wade Belak, Marc Potvin, and Rick Rypien certainly gives us reason to wonder whether there is a connection between playing a physical role and depression.

Boogaard was 28 when he died of an accidental drug and alcohol overdose while recovering from a concussion. Researchers at Boston University studied his brain after his death and reported that it showed early signs of the degenerative brain disease Chronic Traumatic Encephalopathy (CTE).

The BU study showed Boogaard's CTE was more advanced than you would have expected to see in an athlete his age.

Belak was 35 and Rypien was 27 when they allegedly committed suicide. Rypien had battled depression for years, and Belak also suffered from it.

Bob Probert died of a heart attack, but researchers at Boston University also studied his brain and found evidence of CTE.

None of that surprised me because I've had a feeling for several years that my brain was feeling the impact of playing more than a decade in the NHL. I've just had a sense that my brain wasn't normal. I can't explain it, but I know something isn't quite right. I am just foggier than I should be at my age.

Obviously my addiction probably has played a role, but there is certainly evidence today that suggests that constant trauma to your brain can have staggering consequences.

Boogaard had 67 NHL fights, and showed degenerative brain damage. I had exactly twice that many. When you count my minor league fights, I've had 184 pro fights, and that doesn't count the preseason fights. I had 68 fighting majors over my first two seasons of professional hockey.

I was never knocked out in a fight, and I was never officially diagnosed with a documented concussion as a result of a fight. The only time a doctor told me I had a concussion came after Gary Galley checked me from behind during a game in Philadelphia.

Other than that, the only serious injury I got from a fight was slicing some tendons punching Mark Tinordi.

But over the last decade, it seems as if there has been more discussion about the accumulative effect of blows to the head. The NHL is much more cautious about head trauma now. Doctors seem to do a better job today of diagnosing and understanding concussions. The league has protocols in place designed to strengthen the diagnostic process.

Given what we now know about head trauma, it makes me wonder what my career did to my brain. At best, we can say we are not really sure. At worst, we can say it puts me at greater risk for brain-related problems in the future.

You don't have to be a fucking doctor to look around and see that there have been a significant number of tough guys who have had a variety of serious issues.

Tough-guy Chris Nilan was recently featured in the documentary *The Last Gladiators,* and he has battled drug addiction for many years.

Tough-guy Marc Potvin, who played with me in Adirondack, committed suicide after his playing career was over. His death stunned me because he had been one of my mentors in my first year of professional hockey. We would always talk about hockey, fighting, and life. He was one of the veterans who taught me how to be smart about my fights. I remember when I heard of his death I tried to convince myself there was foul play involved because it didn't make any sense to me that he would kill himself. The Potvin I knew wouldn't kill himself.

But today I have a better understanding of how depression works and how torturous it can be on a human being.

Right before I started my professional hockey career in 1992, NHL tough-guy John Kordic died of a drug overdose.

Is there a connection between depression and head trauma? I'm no medical expert, but common sense would suggest there is.

I know there is a connection between fighting and self-medicating. When you are fighting in the NHL on a regular basis you look for ways to ease the pain or to reduce the anxiety. Drinking often seems like the answer, even though it truly isn't. You want to be able to turn your mind off. Being an NHL fighter is a stressful occupation. You live with anxiety for an entire season because you are constantly thinking about who you might have to fight in the next game. Imagine if you had to go to work every day wondering if this is a day when you might have to have your face stitched up or suffer a concussion or break your hand or have your nose broken. You also have to worry about fighting at the right time, because if you fight at the wrong time you could end up with the coach pissed off at you.

At no point did one of my coaches ever order me to fight, though I always understood when it was time to drop the gloves. But some fighters struggle to know when they should fight and when they shouldn't, and that causes even more stress.

There are other concerns which fans don't know about, such as the unspoken code of conduct that most fighters follow.

Sometimes you have to fight the opposing tough guy because he needs a bout just to prove his value to the team.

That kind of request came to me from Calgary Flames tough-guy Paul Kruse at the most inopportune time at the Saddledome.

The night before the game, I had gotten hammered with Paul Coffey and Sheldon Kennedy. The next day I was nursing a killer hangover. I could play, but I certainly wasn't in the mood to be fighting.

As we lined up for a faceoff, Kruse says, "I'm trying to stay in the line-up. Do you think we can go?"

"Yeah, sure," I said.

Before my brain realized that I had agreed to fight, Kruse had hit me five times. That's how groggy I was.

I remember thinking, *Ah shit, I'm in a fight.*

That fight wasn't the longest fight of my career, but it sure seemed like it.

The point is that the fighter's job is far more complicated than just dropping the gloves and swinging away. The work taxes you as much mentally as physically.

Certainly, I'm not suggesting that there isn't fun associated with being an NHL enforcer. Tough guys are often some the funniest guys in the league. We all had a collection of insults and one-liners that we used in the build-up to fights. Some fighters would do their version of stand-up comedy to get a fight started.

Many of us actually got along away from the rink. One of my favorite lighthearted moments with an enforcer came when the Red Wings were at home facing the Calgary Flames and Sandy McCarthy and I got into a stare down about who was going to leave the ice last in the warm-up. Most Detroit fans remember that it was part of superstition, or pregame ritual, to be the last player to leave the ice.

It's what I did, just part of the idea that it was my job to make sure that everything was okay. I would wait at the gate for the second-to-last guy to leave. I wanted him to know that I was staying with him. It's like the military phrase "I've got your six."

The problem was that on this night McCarthy had the same idea. He and I were both stalling waiting for the other guy to leave. He was shooting pucks into the net. I was shooting pucks. I tossed pucks in the crowd. It was a test of our patience and willpower.

I'm sure that Detroit Zamboni driver Al Sobotka was growing impatient because he had a schedule to keep in order for the game to start on time.

Finally, McCarthy and I were both at our respective exits staring at one another. We both started laughing. What no one realized was that we knew each other. We'd been in an All-Star Game together as players, and we'd been roommates.

No end was in sight, so I made a hand-signal to him that we should settle it with a game of rock-paper-scissor. He laughed, but agreed.

I went rock. He went paper. Paper covers rock. He won. I left the ice first. A bet is a bet, particularly when it is among honorable tough guys.

In hindsight, I have positive feelings about the NHL and NHL Players' Association drug program. The doctors in the program are only trying to help the athletes, often before the athlete knows how much trouble he is in.

My only issue with the NHL's drug policy is its position on legitimate, necessary prescription drugs, such as Adderall. The only time during my career that I felt normal was when I was taking that drug for my ADHD.

The problem is that Adderall contains a combination of amphetamine and dextroamphetamine. Those two substances are central nervous system stimulants and they are considered performance enhancing drugs. They are banned for athletes.

It seems immoral to deny a needed drug to an athlete who is under the care of a physician who determines he or she needs that drug.

When I had to go off Adderall, my need for weed became more acute. When I smoked weed I didn't feel as anxious. I felt more in control. Marijuana is not on the banned list because it is not a performance enhancing drug.

I faced many drug tests in my career. At one point, I even tried to use the famed Whizzinator to beat the system.

It's basically a rubber penis, and then you fill it with synthetic urine and then you whip that out and fill the cup. Even if someone is assigned to watch, it looks like you are holding your real dick.

I paid a few hundred dollars for the set-up, and another $20 for the synthetic urine. The Whizzinator gained notoriety when former NFL running back Onterrio Smith was caught with the device in an airport in 2005. Actor Tom Sizemore also got caught trying to beat a drug test with one.

You can add me to the list of people who were caught, although my detection was never revealed by the media.

My problem was that the synthetic urine ruined the testing machine. The NHL fined me $20,000.

I flunked many drug tests in my career, but never for performance enhancing drugs. After a while, I didn't even care if the league knew I was smoking pot.

I specifically remember telling the NHLPA doctors, "I'm gonna smoke weed, because if I don't, I feel like I'm gonna kill someone."

Now that I'm 40, I can feel the physical price I paid for being an NHL fighter. The impact on your body is real and long-lasting.

As a result of my long NHL career, I have a body that screams at me every day. I'm in constant pain. But I refuse to take pain pills, other than over-the-counter relievers such as ibuprofen, Tylenol, or other non-narcotics that doctors prescribe.

But given my addiction, my general rule is that I only seek drug relief when my pain is debilitating.

Even when I had major dental work, I only took prescription medicine for a couple of days, out of fear that I would become dependent on it.

Prescription narcotics are far easier to abuse than most people realize. My alcohol addiction causes me enough problems. I don't want to travel down a different addiction road.

There is no doubt in my mind that Rypien, Belak, and Boogaard were searching for ways to treat their pain. I watched Bob Probert trying to deaden his pain with opioids.

Drugs like Vicodin and oxycodone, when abused, lead to addiction. I've read about former pro athletes succumbing to their addictions through suicide or accidental overdose. What they were really doing was self-medicating. I don't want that to happen to me. That's why I run from pills.

One of the issues facing former pro athletes is that they have no medical insurance when they leave the game, and some don't have the money to buy medical insurance.

I explained what happened to my money, and I accept the blame for my situation. But there are also players who were non-stars who simply didn't make enough money to be set for life. They get done with their careers after bouncing from the American Hockey League to the NHL and back again. They're over 30 and they have no money and no idea what to do next. It's like they're starting over at a time when most people their age have an established career path, and without any work history or skillset.

Then there are athletes like me who have physical issues. I'm in the process of filing for disability and the Workers Compensation for Professional Athletes. But that is difficult to attain. My wife, Sheryl, and I are plowing through the paperwork process now.

Sheryl is a registered nurse and she warns me every day about the impact my addiction has on my liver. When she agreed to be with me, she made me swear off ever taking narcotics.

I use marijuana for pain. Thank God it's legal in Michigan. I smoke regularly, just as if I'm a terminal cancer patient. It's what gets me through the days.

For a lengthy period, I had so much back and shoulder pain that I couldn't sleep. I was constantly in emergency rooms, and the Detroit Red Wings doctors worked with me free of charge. The pain was so bad that I didn't even feel some of the long needles they were sticking in me. When it was concluded that surgery was my only option, Sheryl convinced me to try a chiropractor. We headed first to the Red Wings chiropractor, Dr. Bloom. He began to work with me, and the pain began to lesson. He gave me a neck-stretching device. It helped a bit, but I was still a mess.

It's difficult to explain how much pain I was experiencing. The pain was excruciating to the point that it made me sick to my stomach. Once, when I was having an X-ray done on my shoulder, the repositioning of my shoulder caused so much pain that I began vomiting uncontrollably. I threw up everywhere.

The X-ray technicians were both stunned and grossed out. As a nurse, my wife was unfazed. She asked for towels and cleaned up the entire area. She understood the pain I was experiencing.

This happened in the summer of 2012, and later that month I was attending a celebrity golf tournament in Saginaw, Michigan, when I was debilitated by staggering pain in my shoulder and back.

I called Sheryl to pick me up early, and she was immediately concerned by my symptoms. Within moments she was on the phone to doctors at her hospital, and they expressed concern that I may be experiencing a heart attack or an aortic aneurism. We drove straight to emergency room.

Because she'd worked there for many years she knew the doctors and nurses and they brought me in the back door to prevent me from being hassled in the waiting room by fans while I was waiting to be admitted.

When nurses pegged my blood pressure at 178/128, doctors immediately began to treat me as though I were having a heart attack.

But tests revealed it was not a heart attack. Doctors concluded that my blood pressure simply reflected the pain my body was enduring. As I told the doctors, I have a high pain threshold. So when I say I'm in pain—it's bring-you-to-your-knees pain.

Finally, Sheryl convinced me to go see chiropractor Dr. Dan Wild, who was located in her hometown of Clare, Michigan. Sheryl had been his patient since she was 15. He'd traveled all over the world learning advanced chiropractic techniques.

He examined me for about five or 10 minutes, stretching and lengthening me as he progressed through his examination. Then he stopped manipulating my body and said, "Ah, here is the problem." What he discovered was that my spine had rotated and was pinching the nerves in my back. He turned my head to the right and adjusted me in between my upper shoulders and for the first time in months the pain disappeared. Instantly, I got feeling back in my fingertips. He said, "Darren, you can bring your head back to the center." But I was afraid that if I did the pain would return. I just wanted to sit like that and relish in the euphoric feeling of NO PAIN!

When I came back to the center the pain was still gone. There was no surgery. No one was cutting me. Dr. Wild fixed me, for a $30 office visit, without taking any X-rays. Now every time we are in Clare, his office is my first stop.

That's not to say my physical problems are permanently resolved. Far from it. The left arm that I used to pound Claude Lemieux and many other NHL combatants now can't be raised above my left shoulder. Excruciating pain shoots through my body when I attempt to move the shoulder normally. Doctors say that I have arthritis and a very shallow socket because my shoulder was dislocated too many times.

A bulging disc and inflamed nerves cause problems in my back. The pain is often unbearable. Cortisone shots and Toradol injections provide minimal—and temporary—relief. For an eight-week stretch I slept every night in a recliner because that was the only position that allowed some measure of comfort.

My hands are so swollen and disfigured that they don't even look human.

I can forecast the weather better than any meteorologist. When my hands bloat and ache more than usual, I know that it's going to rain. I can feel the arthritis winning the battle in the joints.

Doctors have told me I will need major surgery to maintain normal usage of my fingers within a few years.

Each of the scars on my body is its own story. Each time I look at my pinky and ring finger I remember pulling two of Mark Tinordi's teeth out of my fingers after a fight years ago. I severed an artery in that fight, which required surgery to fix.

On most days, I don't even notice the scars on my forehead and under my eyes, but on other days seeing them reminds me of the many battles I fought in an NHL sweater.

My nose was broken seven times, and is crooked to the point of being cartoonish.

When I'm teasing or harassing my wife, she often responds, "If you keep it up, I'll straighten that nose for you."

My scarred chin and lips and false tooth tell a story of the days when hockey was more old school than it is today.

The story of my false tooth actually began when I was nine years old and swimming in my grandparents' pool in Woodslee. I jumped off the side railings and came down tooth-first on my aunt's head. That front tooth went flying out of my mouth. Then, in 2000–01, St. Louis Blues defenseman Alexander Khavanov got a little nervous when I came in to hit him and he brought his stick up to protect himself, knocking out the replacement tooth.

I needed dental surgery and had a temporary replacement put in. Soon after, the replacement tooth was knocked out. Then the replacement to that replacement got knocked out. When it happened a third time, I figured enough was enough. I wasn't going back to the dentist a fourth time.

Using pliers, I removed the posts from my mouth after Game 2 of the playoff series against Vancouver in 2002.

"I'll get this fucking tooth fixed after I'm done playing," I announced to my teammates.

That's when I started viewing my missing tooth as a championship symbol like the Stanley Cup and the championship ring.

People always tried to convince me to have it replaced, but I never wanted to do it because it would be like erasing a great memory.

But my other teeth began causing problems, and my amazing dentist friend Demi Kazanis looked into my mouth and told me I needed major dental surgery or else I was going to start having serious problems.

She also discovered that I had a genetic trait where my teeth are fused to the jaw bone, so I never really "lost" a tooth—they were broken off from my jaw. It took many months and several different tooth extractions, root canals, and finally a temporary bridge. My permanent bridge came and I had one final implant and boom—my teeth look great again! My dentist and my wife have become best friends; Sheryl says she's my twin sister, the female version of me. And when we hang out together, it is very clear that Sheryl is right. Demi has such a huge heart for giving; she donates huge amounts of money to different charities every month. She did my teeth for free. She also donated to this book project. She believes in me and my story. We are so blessed to have her in our life. She has been through as much in her life as I have in mine. I'm very lucky to call her my friend.

Still, I have no regrets about how I made my living. I enjoyed being an NHL player, and I liked the physical aspect of the game.

People often ask me where I think I would be had I not been an NHL player. I think they believe I will say that I would be healthier or less broken down if I hadn't played this sport.

But what I really believe is that if I hadn't played in the NHL I might be dead by now.

It was being an NHL player that prevented me from being wilder than I was. There was too much money at stake for me to completely let myself go. I didn't want to lose my job.

Plus, I was playing on a team, and my teammates were always looking out for me, trying to convince me to slow down. As wild as I was, I still had boundaries. There were lines I wouldn't cross.

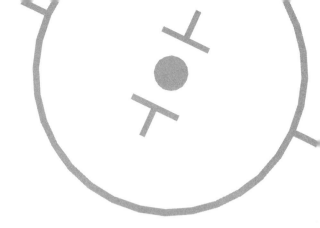

Chapter 15

How I Met My Wife

"She wore blue Jeans and a Rosary,
believed in God and believed in me"

—"Blue Jeans and a Rosary"
Kid Rock

How I Met My Wife

Because of my image as a wild party guy, people will believe anything they hear about my life.

That allows Sheryl and I to have fun making my life seem wilder than it really was. We've been asked so many times how we met that we've started to make up shit for the sake of telling a good story.

People want to hear a crazy-ass tale that involves sex, drugs, violence, or rock 'n' roll, so we give it to them.

When fans ask how we met, we take turns fabricating a story. I'm actually impressed about how creative our stories have become.

We have told people that Sheryl was a Las Vegas stripper and that I met her in a VIP room or during a raunchy pole dance. We have told people that she was a high-priced escort and she showed up one night at my door and it was love at first sight.

We've also told people that we met in a meet-and-greet line, or that I fell in love with her when I heard her sing karaoke. One of my favorites is that she was in a bar and coldcocked a drunken fan who was talking shit about me.

There is also a story about me being badly injured in a bar fight and Sheryl being the nurse that took care of me in the emergency room.

The truth is that Sheryl has never even been to Las Vegas, and the only accurate fact in all of our stories is that Sheryl is a registered nurse.

At the very least, the story about Sheryl pounding a guy in a bar fight has the potential to be true because she is tougher than I am. She also might confront someone who was spreading lies about me. My wife's true background is that she worked at a law firm while attending college to earn a nursing degree and her many certifications. There is no stripper's pole in her history.

We met in 2010 while I was in the midst of a fresh addiction: Golden Tee.

I had officially retired in 2009, and my life started to go down the sink-hole immediately. After contributing to a Stanley Cup victory in 2008, I'd hoped to play a more prominent role in 2008–09. But it never happened. I had more injuries, and ended up playing in only 13 games for the Red Wings that season.

Although the Red Wings made it back to the Stanley Cup Final, I didn't play in the postseason.

Not surprising, I actually had more fun that season playing in the American League with Grand Rapids. In 19 games, I had five goals and 11 points. I played for coach Curt Fraser, a no-nonsense coach who liked to say guys were "playing soft as grapes."

That is now among my favorite coaching lines.

After I quit, my life became a week-long party. At the time, I was living in a townhouse in Troy, Michigan. My neighbors didn't much like me because my lifestyle wasn't suitable for family viewing. They didn't like the hours I kept.

I would be up at noon, then off to a shithole bar to play Golden Tee and get stinkin' drunk. I would close down the bar at 2:00 AM and then move the party back to my townhouse until I passed out with one of the five puck-whores I was seeing at the time. I referred to my collection of women as my "3:00 AM girlfriends."

Then I'd wake up the next day and do it all over again. Wash. Rinse. Repeat. It was like I was living the movie, *Groundhog Day*. Only Bill Murray and Andie MacDowell weren't in my version.

My posse was a sketchy group of low-life human beings that included a drug dealer that I knew from my days when I was heavy into using ecstasy. He and his wife hung out with me all of the time. I never quite understood what their relationship was all about. He and his wife were Red Wings fans and they did everything for me, including cleaning my house, doing my laundry, and keeping me well-stocked with drugs.

The woman would meet with my cocaine dealer to pick up my drugs. She would pick up my "3:00 AM dates" and bring them to my house and then drove them home when I was done with them. She made sure that all of those women thought they were the only woman I was hanging out with, even though I didn't care if they knew there were other women or not.

Eventually I began to trust the drug dealer's woman like she was one of my best friends. I gave her my credit card and told her to pay my bills for me.

What I didn't realize was that she was using my credit card to pay her bills and to go shopping. She robbed me blind.

But I was clueless because the three of us would sit up and do drugs all night. One of them was always with me, and not because I asked them to be. I was too stoned to notice that these two people were using me. My life was a mess, and I was about to meet a woman who would help me see that.

First, I had to meet a dude named Bart. We met because he liked to play Golden Tee after he got out of work.

The first night we met he sang Johnny Cash's "Folsom Prison Blues," and it was the best karaoke rendition I had ever heard. It was awesome. We became instant friends.

The interesting aspect of our friendship is that Bart didn't follow sports. He knew nothing about sports in general, or the NHL specifically. He didn't know Darren McCarty as a member of the Grind Line and he didn't care about the Detroit Red Wings.

He's a businessman. He had no agenda other than he liked being my friend. There was no hidden agenda. We were just friends with some common interests. One of his interests that became one of my interests was the huge Irish festival in his hometown of Clare, Michigan. I was excited to get out of the Troy area for the weekend, so on March 12, 2010, Bart and me and his two friends, both named Mark, all jumped in my beat-up minivan and headed north on a two-hour trip to Clare.

After we arrived, I walked into the big old hotel in the center of the city and the first person I saw was a very tall, slim woman walking through the back lobby with a guy who looked like he could be her brother. She had long, dark, almost black hair and huge dark brown eyes.

She didn't even look our way, or so I thought.

"Bart, who the fuck is that woman?" I asked.

"You mean Sheryl?" he said. "That's my wife."

My jaw dropped, leaving me standing there with my mouth hanging open.

Bart is maybe 5'5" on his tallest day, and Sheryl is 6' without shoes on. Within a few seconds, my instincts told me there was no fucking way that Bart and Sheryl were a couple.

"You wish she was your wife," I said, laughing. "In your dreams, maybe, she is your wife."

He confessed immediately that they were not married, but that they were friends. Because of their dramatic height difference, it had become a running joke in the town that they were married.

"She's actually no one's wife," Bart offered. "She hates men. She's unattainable. Don't even try it."

He pointed out that the mammoth man next to her was her best friend.

"He's as crazy as you are, so don't try anything," Bart said.

Telling me that Sheryl was "unattainable" was like placing a high-tech safe in a safe cracker's living room and telling him not to try to open it.

"Challenge accepted," I told Bart.

He just laughed, not truly believing I was going to make much of an effort.

I pressed Bart for more details, and he told me that Sheryl had been divorced for 11 years and that she had five crazy older brothers, one of whom was nicknamed "Dig Your Grave Dave."

Her best friend was known as the town's fighter. From the stories I was told, he was clearly a bad ass.

"You guys are very much alike," Bart said.

The more I heard about Sheryl, the more intrigued I became.

Bart approached Sheryl and they hugged. Then Bart suggested that everyone come up to our hotel room to "get away from the crowd."

Much later, I learned that Sheryl had noticed me when I came in the door. Apparently, there aren't many men over 6' in town. Plus, I weighed 235 pounds.

According to Sheryl, she asked her giant man-friend who the guy was with Bart.

"Do you mean the guy with the missing tooth?" the friend said. "How the hell should I know? And since when do you care who some guy is?"

A little while later, Sheryl and her friend showed up at our room. The two Marks also had invited some friends, and before long our hotel room looked like the Post Bar on a Saturday night.

Sheryl sat stone sober in a chair on one side of the room, watching everyone getting liquored up. I sat on the opposite side of the room, studying her.

She was gorgeous. On one hand, she looked like a prissy woman dressed in her extra-long, blinged-out, expensive jeans and her black, trendy, super-high heels. She wore no rings on her fingers and wore only small diamond earrings. She also wore a big rosary around her neck, and the beads lay perfectly on her chest.

As I watched her interact with her friends, she had smart, witty responses. She was funny, and didn't take shit from anyone.

She never moved off her chair, and yet she felt like the center of the party. Everyone came over to talk to her. She was never alone for a single moment. I was fascinated by her. I was ridiculously attracted to her. I had to meet her. I watched her for more than an hour. When someone from hotel security knocked on the door, I saw my chance to meet her.

I pointed at Sheryl and yelled, "Bart, you and her, get into the bathroom. I don't want security to see me here. I don't need the drama of everyone knowing I'm here."

Sheryl rarely drinks, is always sober, and is known as someone who protects her crazy friends. She rolled her eyes at the insistence that we needed to hide, but she went along with the request.

She ended up sitting on the shower seat and I parked on the toilet as Bart leaned on the sink.

We sat in there and talked for hours. But the minute I started flirting, she poured cold water on my advances.

"Let's make something clear right off the bat," she said. "I have no intention of dating you or anyone else. I don't want to be married. It's not my desire to be any man's wife, and I don't want to have any more children."

She believed her speech would send me running to the hills. Instead, I fell in love. She was my kind of woman.

I stopped my obvious flirting and started listening. In our bathroom conversation I found out that she was raised spending her summers working on the family's quarter-horse farm. She has five brothers and five sisters and they'd race the horses every summer. She's an avid bow hunter. She outshoots the boys. She educated me about bows and hunting equipment and "peep sites" and "releases" and other hunting stuff. I asked her questions just to watch her answer them. She is definitely one of the guys. I learned that her father is a down-home Southern boy from Georgia who speaks with a drawl and her Italian mother was raised in the hills of Tennessee. She loves country music *and* rock 'n' roll. I studied her—the bathroom was filled with the smell of her perfume, which I later learned was appropriately named "Beautiful." I remember thinking that it was the most amazing smell I'd ever smelled on the most amazing woman I'd ever met. You'd never believe looking at her that she is a country girl, with her long, expensive pleated jeans and high heels. I never knew country girls looked like her. She told me that her mother is an evangelist, and Sheryl had to attend bible studies once a week in her home and went to Church three times a week.

The home had one television with three channels, and Sheryl knew absolutely nothing about hockey.

She'd been married before, and had two children, but she'd been divorced for 11 years.

She had no idea who I was, and I could tell right away that she wouldn't give a shit even if she did. I made no mention of my NHL background. I put away my "smooth talking game" and was just myself, minus any reference to hockey.

I didn't want to bring up hockey because our connection seemed pure and real. I felt like I did when I was growing up in Leamington, before I became No. 25.

Sheryl seemed different than most women I'd known. I didn't want to leave the bathroom. I was afraid that the minute we walked out of the bathroom she was going to disappear into the night.

A plan was hatched to head to a bowling alley bar, and we exited the bathroom against my better judgment. I grabbed her hand and rushed out into the crowd.

"Don't let go of my hand," I said. "Don't lose me."

I meant that long-term as well as short-term. I was smitten like a schoolboy.

Unfortunately, some Red Wings fans recognized me and yelled my name.

We arrived at the car, and Sheryl was the only sober person available to drive. It looked like a clown car as we packed in.

"What's that about?" Sheryl asked.

"What was what about?" I said, even though I knew what she was talking about.

A voice emerged from the piles of humanity in the car, and it was Bart telling me it was time to come clean about my Red Wings past.

When we piled out of her Hummer, I told her that I had been an NHL player.

She laughed, and said, "That's cool, can we go in the bar now?"

It is fair to say her reaction was not the kind of reaction that I usually get when someone finds out I was a professional athlete. To her, it was the same as if I had told her I'd been a banker or a construction worker.

I asked her whether she had heard of either Steve Yzerman or Wayne Gretzky, and she said she had heard of Yzerman and the Red Wings. But she had no other information about professional hockey. None. Zero. I told her I played in the same league with those guys, and somehow we even uncovered the truth that she shared the same birthday as Wayne Gretzky.

She seemed to have no interest in my hockey past or my NHL accomplishments. She didn't care about No. 25. But she seemed to be interested in Darren McCarty. This turned me on.

Sheryl did inform me that she was annoyed that I decided not to reveal my background when we initially met. This was my first notice about how much she reveres honesty and full disclosure in a relationship.

"You should have told me when you were holding me hostage in the bathroom," she said.

"Well, now you know—and now you may understand what it means," I said.

The bowling alley bar was overflowing with people from all over the state for the festival. Apparently, many of them were Red Wings fans. I walked in with my head held high, and soon I was in the midst of an autograph session. It was chaos as people came up to talk to me and to get me to sign whatever they had on them.

Sheryl looked mortified as she witnessed what it's like to be me in a crowd of Detroit fans. I used the craziness to my advantage, telling Sheryl that she needed to stay close to me to help me escape if the crowd became too unruly. She was one of the few sober people in the place, and my request for her help fed into her protective instincts.

She wanted to run, but she couldn't because she felt obligated to serve and protect. We hung out together until the bar closed, and then went back to the pool area at the hotel. We sat at a table until almost dawn.

At that point in my life, my normal game plan would have been to try to get her into my bed. But I knew there was no chance of that happening. After 12 hours of stalking and wooing her, I didn't even have her phone number.

There were plenty of women at the festival that I could have had in my bed that night, but I paid no attention to any of them because I couldn't take my eyes off her.

At 5:00 in the morning, Sheryl said she needed to get some sleep because she was going to be in the parade on a party bus. She had to be there at 8:00 AM.

"I'll be there," I said.

'Yeah, right," she said.

She went to sleep at her sister's house, and when she showed up to get on the bus for the parade, the first person she saw was me. I didn't sleep all night because I was afraid I would miss my opportunity to hang out with her again. I made Bart hang out with me because I knew he could get me where I needed to be for the parade.

I didn't know whether Sheryl was impressed or afraid that she had a lunatic on her hands when she saw me. But I didn't care. I was there with her.

We handed out beads along the parade route, and when it was over Bart and his friends jumped off the bus to start an informal pub crawl. Sheryl said she was riding the bus back to the parade starting point because that was where her truck was parked.

After I jumped off the bus with the boys, I told Bart that I had forgotten my beer holder on the bus. It was a lie. I just wanted to get back on the bus with Sheryl. I told Bart I would meet him later in the bar.

I was actually worried that if I went off with Bart that I would never see Sheryl again. Every bar was packed shoulder-to-shoulder and I thought it was likely that I wouldn't be able to find Sheryl if I allowed her to escape to her truck.

As I walked back to the bus with Sheryl, I pulled my beer holder out of my pocket to show her.

She just shook her head, knowing that it meant another day of having me glued to her. We hung out until 10:00 PM, and then she said she was tired and needed to go home. We had been together for about 43 hours, and I had spent most of them trying to secure her phone number. She would not provide it. She just laughed at my frequent requests.

She walked me back to my room and then let me kiss her. She laughed again at my final request for her number. Then she walked back and faded into the crowd. I went to bed alone and left Clare at 5:00 AM, saddened by the possibility that I might never see her again.

I decided I was not going to allow that to happen.

When I got home I pulled out the computer and, with Bart's help, I found her on Facebook.

"Hi, will you be my friend?" I asked simply.

"Of course, dork," she replied. "Apparently, you didn't find the phone number I stuck in your coat pocket."

In the 42nd hour of our weekend, Sheryl had provided me with her phone number without me realizing what was happening.

I've worked hard to accomplish several goals in my life, but I never worked harder on any endeavor than I did in acquiring her phone number.

We talked daily, and she was interested in me, but she was clearly not interested in my lifestyle. At one point she told me that honesty is the most important standard of any relationship or friendship.

To Sheryl, everything is forgiven as long as someone is fully honest about what he or she has done. Sheryl believes if someone is honest with you than he or she is treating you like an important person in their life. If they are not being honest, then clearly they are not treating you like an important person in their life. Trust, love, and friendship blossom from pure honesty.

Sheryl can forgive the act, but not the lie. She believes that if a man cheats on his wife and comes home and lies about it, then he is saying that his wife is less important than the adultress. If he comes home and confesses the infidelity, then he's saying that the wife is more important than the skank he bedded.

Trust me when I say that Sheryl lives by this standard. I've experienced her forgiveness on so many levels and her forgiveness took away my desire to be the unfaithful person I had always been.

I trusted Sheryl and felt at ease telling her everything about my personal life. She knew about the unsavory women I was bedding. She knew about my low-life friends. She knew about my partying. She knew about my drug problem. She didn't judge me. Instead, she accepted me with my faults. When I told her I was weary of living this way and wanted to be healthy, she said she would help me. Sheryl agreed to be my friend, but repeated in a frank and honest way that she had no desire to be in any kind of a dating or romantic relationship with me.

I believed that I could convince her to date me. It was clear to me that it would mean making changes in my life.

"I need to cut down some trees," I said to her one night. I think she knew what I meant. My life had become overgrown with issues and people who didn't have my best interests at heart. I needed to create a clearing so I could see a future.

What she didn't realize was that what I really needed to do was cut down an entire fucking forest.

Sheryl didn't ask me to change. Not once. But she was the first woman that made me want to change. In the lowest time of my life, she was a friend.

Our relationship grew gradually. I would drive up north to see her, and she started to come down to Troy to hang out.

Early in our friendship, I begged her to have a committed relationship.

"Darren, you're not ready for that yet," she would say very sweetly.

She worked in a hospital, but she would chisel out some time to come down to the Troy area to hang out with me. I'd head up to Clare and Saginaw to see Sheryl on her off days. It was like I was courting her, the way it was done years ago.

Meanwhile, I was trying to knock down the trees that were blocking my growth as a person. On many days, it felt like I was hacking through a rainforest.

It wasn't as if I became a choir boy overnight. I have an addictive personality, and changing my lifestyle wasn't as simple as just telling everyone in my life to go away.

I still partied at the same bars and I saw all the same women. They were persistent, and I wasn't always strong. My heart was with Sheryl, but my cock sometimes had a different agenda.

Had I known that years later these people would stalk and harass Sheryl, I may have given them the Claude Lemieux treatment.

In September 2010, there was an NHL alumni trip to Aspen, Colorado. I wanted to go and I wanted to bring Sheryl with me. By then, we had been "friends" for six months. Sheryl still hadn't decided whether I was ready to take our relationship to a higher level.

There was much begging on my part for her to accompany me on this trip and there was much canceling on her part.

Sheryl went back-and-forth on whether or not she should attend the gathering.

The day before we were to fly to Aspen, Sheryl called her ex-husband to tell him that he didn't have to watch their children that weekend because she had decided not to make the trip.

Her ex-husband, Rob, changed my life because he told Sheryl to give me a chance.

"You have to stop hating men and let one get close to you," he told her. "You deserve to broaden your horizons and have some fun."

She listened to him and reluctantly decided to go on the alumni trip. It was the turning point in our relationship. We say we fell in love on that trip, even though it was love-at-first-sight for me when we met in Clare.

Sheryl says now that when she boarded the plane and saw all of the other former players' wives with their bleach blonde hair, Louis Vuitton luggage, and huge diamond rings, she wanted to "run [her] county bumpkin ass right off the plane and back to the horse barn."

What she couldn't see, and still doesn't today, is that she looks as glamorous as any of them. No one would have known she was a small-town girl if she hadn't told them.

Of course, as soon as Sheryl met everyone, she fit in perfectly. Sheryl and BettyAnne Ogrodnick, the wife of former Red Wing John Ogrodnick, became instant friends. They're like sisters today. BettyAnne stands by Sheryl and mentors her through all of the craziness my "hockey life" brings us. In my opinion, there is no one better to mentor her—the wives and players actually refer to her as "Queen B." We love her and Johnny O very much. I'm honored to wear the same number he wore on his sweater.

By the way, I'm also now friends with Sheryl's ex-husband, the man who helped finally convince Sheryl that she had to take a chance to find some happiness. I will never be able to thank Rob and Bart enough for helping me connect with Sheryl.

My relationship with Sheryl worked because she never sought to control me or change me. She sought to help me. She has marched to hell and back with me, and she showed me how my life could be better if I made safer and smarter choices.

She stands next to me as I face this demon monster of addiction, never judging and always accepting me.

After we were in a committed relationship, she arrived at my house after working a 13-hour shift and found one of my sketchy friends at my table with a plate of cocaine in front of him.

"Hi," she said. "I'll see you later."

I grabbed her and begged her not to leave. "I've counted down the hours until you got here," I said.

I knew I needed her. I knew she was the best friend I had. I didn't want to fuck up this relationship. I wanted her to know how hard I was trying.

"Darren," she said, "I will never tell what you can or cannot do, I will never tell you who can or cannot be in your life, but I can tell you who and what I won't be around. This is your choice."

As she walked out the door, one member of my entourage raced past her at 100 miles an hour. He was never in my life again.

Sheryl was more upset about the loser being in my house than the drugs. I chose her over everything else in my life. She helped me redefine a new normal in my life. She helped me leave the world of whores, drugs, and poor choices. She helped eradicate the maggot population in my life that was sucking the life out of me.

She helped gain control over the No. 25 beast. He had become a monster to the point that his important friends didn't always recognize him.

In the heat of the moment I used a hockey stick to clear the human trash from my house—Sheryl didn't flinch. When the explosive moment was over, she removed the hockey stick from my hand and told me to go lie down.

While I napped to find some peace, she cleaned my house. All of the rubbish was removed from my life. She helped eliminate the mess I created.

Sheryl stood by me at a time when others might have run away. She saw me turn over my pool table with one hand. She saw me throw a beer glass through a 55-inch television. When she was stalked and harassed by the people I was trying to remove from my life, she never backed down. When she became the target of their rage and anger she showed no fear.

She has helped me navigate back toward a more normal life. I'd ignored life's chores for a few years. When she met me, I wasn't even officially divorced from Anna because I hadn't signed the divorce papers. I had no idea that I was still married. My driver's license had expired and my immigration filings were out-of-date. The paperwork of my life was a mess.

Sheryl pulled me back from a dark place. She does the job in real life that I did in the NHL—she is my protector. Sheryl understands that alcoholism is a disease and she stands by me and fights it head on. I often ask her how she can love me so much. I asked her once why she doesn't judge me like everyone in my past has. She answered, "Would I judge how you handle your pain if you had cancer? No way, I'd be there through the suffering of that disease, too, and we'd kick cancer's ass the same way we're beating this alcohol monster." Thank God we're both fighters.

She's a strong person, and she's the one person I wouldn't want to go toe-to-toe with. Her Italian mother taught her strength and loyalty, and now I'm the beneficiary of those traits. She's my nurse, my ally, my lover, and my best friend.

She loves me as Darren—not as former NHL player Darren McCarty. She doesn't even know me as the hockey player.

"I wish you were just a retired General Motors worker," she always says.

Sheryl may never get used to strangers walking up to me and starting conversations about the Red Wings glory days. To me, it's mostly fun. I loved being a player and I loved relating to the fans. And over time she's started to have some fun with it, too. There's no point in running from it.

Sheryl and I were married in 2012 at sunset at Clearwater Beach, Florida, the day after my 40th birthday. It was the best birthday gift that I ever received.

"Both my broken wings, every single piece of everything I am, yeah she knows the man I ain't, she forgives me when I can't, the devil man, no, he don't stand a chance cause she loves me like Jesus does"

—"Like Jesus Does"
Eric Church

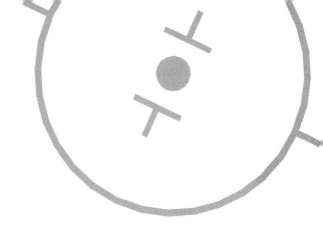

Chapter 16
The Y Chromosome
(Here you go, Jimbo)

"Girls, Girls, Girls"

—"Girls, Girls, Girls"
Mötley Crüe

The Y Chromosome
(Here you go, Jimbo)

For a normal man, remaining monogamous is a chore. But for a pro athlete with an addictive personality, it's impossible.

That's not me offering an excuse for my behavior throughout my NHL career. It's just me being honest. This is me trying to understand why I did the things I did. I don't like to live with regret, but I've found a lot of it in the way I've treated women, particularly the women who were close to me.

In researching this chapter, I came upon these quotes:

"Monogamy was created for human morality—it isn't 'natural' for us as humans, it goes against our genetics, but society and religion steer us away from nature. With age comes maturity, boys turn to men, but the hunt never stops." —former NFL player Chad Johnson

"I made my share of mistakes. People can look at that as what *not* to do, and if they chose to make fun of it, that's fine, I can't control that, I *can* control myself. And at that point in my life, I wasn't even able to do that." —golfer Tiger Woods

"I was going through a pretty rebellious period where it didn't matter what [my wife] Karin said, I was going to do the opposite. I was really self-absorbed. You keep getting temptation thrown in your face and eventually you're going to slip up." —former MLB player Chipper Jones

"I was a guy with too many options. Choosing to be with some of those women, well, that's on me. In my mind, I never did it disrespectfully, but obviously I shouldn't have done it all."—former NBA player Shaquille O'Neal

When I read those quotes and review my own life, I have a heavy heart. I offer this chapter with a loud sigh because this is not an easy topic to discuss. But since I have been providing everyone the unvarnished truth about my life, it would be an injustice to not include a chapter about my infidelity. Unfortunately, womanizing is part of the story of my life. My journey has included frequent bad decision making.

When I started playing in the NHL, my first observation about women was that some of them were crazy for their pursuit of pro athletes. I am speaking only about my personal experiences here, but over the years I've interacted with other professional athletes and it's my opinion that NHL players are the *most* monogamous of professional athletes. I don't know why. It's an observation, not a scientific study. I base some of it on what I read in the media about divorcing athletes and athletes paying child support for children they fathered.

Also, I believe today's athletes are more faithful to their wives. Maybe they learned from the mistakes the athletes of my generation made. Because my problems have sometimes played out in the newspaper, everyone has had front-row seats to my soap opera life. Maybe some athletes have learned by looking at the price I've paid for my infidelity and bad decisions. I hope that's true. It would offer some consolation if some good has come out of the mess I made of my life.

I think today's athletes are marrying smarter. They're getting married later. I know players today who won't date a woman who doesn't have some career of her own. Today, athletes all discuss pre-nuptial agreements and they aren't afraid of asking their fiancée to sign one.

It's a different world now. I think athletes are more careful trying to find the right woman. It took me three times to get it right. I learned. Others have learned as well. There seems to be more longevity in athletes' marriages today.

I'm certainly not saying that today's athletes are all perfect, nor am I saying that all athletes from my era were running around on their wives. That would not be true. Even in my era, the majority of men were good, decent, faithful family men. But I wasn't in that group of faithful family men.

The truth is that I had a difficult time dealing with the temptations of the women who were attracted to professional athletes. I'm going to set the record straight about me, not anyone else who played in the NHL in my era. If they want to talk about what they were doing, or who they were doing, they can write their own books. This chapter is exclusively about my exploits, and the mistakes I made.

For a long time, I believed wives lived in denial about the temptation that athletes faced on the road. As an athlete, I'd spent many, many days on the road traveling without any checks and balances. No one knew what I was doing on the road, not even my closest teammates. I was making a boat-load of money and felt like a modern day gladiator. That lifestyle brought temptations that I couldn't resist. Frankly, I made no effort to resist them. To me, I had received an open invitation to stray. I was out "living the dream" while my wife was at home turning a blind eye. I believed she was happy being married to the "lifestyle." She didn't see, or didn't want to see, what I was doing on the road. When a woman marries an athlete, she has to know she is marrying into a culture where there are always women chasing after their husbands.

I'm certainly not suggesting that wives are doing anything to deserve their husbands' infidelity. I'm suggesting that they often ignore the signs of infidelity because they don't want to face the consequences of confrontation or divorce.

Often, these are millionaire couples who both have much to lose through a divorce. The wife often is faced with the emotional choice of confronting a cheating husband or the economic choice of letting it go to preserve the family's affluent lifestyle.

Sometimes, keeping a relationship intact isn't about love. It's about money. We often read about athletes caught cheating. The list of athletes who are unfaithful husbands is long, and I bet there are others whose wives give them a pass because they don't want to deal with the financial consequences of confronting them.

No one wants to hear that said, but it's the truth.

To be very clear, let me say that I accept full blame for my philandering ways. I am guilty of promiscuous behavior, but the women involved were just as guilty. I never took advantage of anyone. They knew everything about me when they became involved with me, including the fact that I was married. I was a whore. They were whores. In the end, we both were trying to fill some void by being together.

My first sexual experience came when I was 16 years old and playing Junior B hockey in Peterborough. Although at the time the legal drinking age was 19 in Canada, I had secured a fake ID that allowed me to enter bars with my older buddies.

One night, I met a 20-year-old woman at a bar. Her name was Kim. She was a 5'8", 120-pound young beauty. She was a brunette, and at that age I knew just enough to know that I preferred brunettes.

Kim was there with her sister, and they invited me back to their house because their parents weren't home.

I lost my virginity that night to Kim. I had no idea what the fuck I was doing, but I sure liked what was happening. She and I dated—if you can call it that—for five or six months. When my parents came to their cottage in Peterborough one weekend, I even introduced her as my girlfriend.

I'm reasonably sure my mom was mortified that her 16-year-old son was dating a then-21-year-old woman. I bet my dad was proud though.

Ten years later, Kim stopped me after the Red Wings had played the Maple Leafs in Toronto. She asked me if I remembered her. I honestly didn't. She had to refresh my memory. It was embarrassing for just a moment. It was strange seeing her standing there with her husband and two young children.

She was my first sexual experience, and that opened up Pandora's box. It occurred to me after spending time with Kim that being an athlete could open doors as well as girls' legs.

After I played Junior B in Peterborough, I came home that summer as a teenager on the prowl for sexual conquests. Believe me when I say

I made the rounds with the girls in my tiny town of Leamington. My parents had transformed our garage into a spacious bedroom with a sliding door to the outside. That was my room when I was home.

My stepdad got up for work every day at 5:00 in the morning. Many times that summer, I had barely slipped through the sliding door, and dove onto the bed before he flicked on that light to make sure I'd made it home. I was definitely out and about every night with various girls and women from my community.

When I played in the OHL for the Belleville Bulls I was in a serious relationship with Cheryl, the woman who would become my first wife in 1992.

I didn't even stay faithful through the innocent honeymoon period of that relationship. My mother once walked in on me when I had a girl in my bed at the family home in Leamington. I had snuck her in the night before.

My mom was unhappy that her son had brought an unknown woman into her home for sex. But she was more devastated over the fact that I was cheating on Cheryl. She pointed out that my little sister could've walked in and then told Cheryl, who was still living in Belleville.

I always had a problem with monogamy and should've realized that before I ever married. When I was playing for Belleville I had at least 10 sexual partners even though I was in a supposed "committed" relationship. I'd attend parties, or hangouts, and women just flocked to the hockey players, especially to me because I was considered a high-end NHL prospect. Plus, I had a cool mullet.

When I finally became an NHL player my opportunities for sexual experiences went to a whole new level. It's hard to explain my mindset at the time, but it suffices to say that I had a warped approach to my marriage.

If you value the sanctity of marriage, as I do today, you will not like this story. I don't like telling this story, but I want to be honest about how I lived my life. Maybe someone will learn from my experiences.

I thought of marriage as a house. I looked at my wife as if she was my mother—or my warden. Our home was like a hotel and she was the keeper of the inn.

To me, marriage was not about sex and romance. It was a business partnership, the constant discussion of money and bills and the logistical decisions about our lives. Then children came along, and that made the business partnership more complicated. That doesn't mean I didn't love my kids, because through all of the ups and downs, I've always loved my kids. But outside the walls of my home, I had another awesome life I was enjoying. I lived a second life in which I had endless money, endless opportunities, endless fun, and endless pussy.

When I returned home to base camp, I could park my car in a safe place and lay in my familiar bed. Being sexually faithful to my wife didn't even seem like a consideration. Frankly, it wasn't an option, considering the opportunities being thrown in my face.

Again, I'm not suggesting for a moment that my actions were justified. I'm explaining the warped vision I had of my marriage.

Women who chased me were relentless, and they still are today. And at the height of my NHL career, there were herds of these women. At every game I played at Joe Louis Arena, there were women sitting in the stands believing they were going to spend the night with Darren McCarty.

My watering holes were well established, and the women who wanted me knew where to find me. When I was drinking—and even when I was sober—I was like hunted prey. I was a rich, horny, well-built professional athlete in the prime of my career, and women seemed to love me.

I fucked women in walk-in coolers, public bathrooms, bar offices, cars, and everywhere else you can imagine. I'm not going to lie about this: it was fun. I felt like I was King of the World. And for some reason the women felt important, too.

Eventually, I discovered there were women who would fly in to cities to meet me when I took road trips. For example, I had a chick in Chicago; I'd leave her a key to my room when I played the Blackhawks, and after the game she'd be in the room, or in a room of her own if I had a roommate. If they weren't from the city I was playing in, they'd fly to meet me there. We'd have sex all night and they'd fly out in the morning. It was funny because when I had roommates and would have to meet the chick in her own room, a few times on the plane the next morning my teammates would be talking about how the person in the next room was having sex so loudly and about the headboard banging on the wall all night. They had no idea it was me. I'd just laugh to myself because they had no clue. These women paid for their own airfare and didn't even want tickets to the game. I kept it very low-key most of the time. It amazes me the lengths women would go to to be able to say they slept with an NHL player. They had to make it very convenient for me or it simply wouldn't happen. "Convenient and relentless" are the two best words to describe them.

During my various surgeries, some of these women would even come to the hospital after my wife left to "take care" of me, if you know what I mean. Even tethered to an IV, I was having sex.

My Detroit teammates were never really sure what was going on because I liked to disappear on the road. I would drop my bag in the room, and then DMac would vanish.

Guys would joke about me having ninja dust or a Houdini act.

I would hang with my Detroit teammates for a while, and then I would stray, like an alley cat on the prowl. Kris Draper never liked that I had two sets of friends—my hockey friends and others. Drapes always thought it was my other friends who were getting me in trouble.

He may have been right, but it was my own doing. I liked to do my own thing, like when I went through my stripper phase.

As an aside, it's true what they say about strip clubs having the best food. I have never once had a bad meal at a strip joint.

I would go to a strip club at 1:00 PM and then stay until 7:00 PM for shift change. I did that to give myself a look at the entire field. Then I would invite two or three of them to a hotel room to take care of business and then I would call taxis to take them wherever they needed to go. Strippers rarely said no to that invitation. Strippers always lined up for the opportunity to go with No. 25.

This happened once or twice a month. If I was pressed for time, I felt like I could go into a club at 5:00 or 6:00 PM and have enough time to chat up the first-shift women before the next shift arrived. Even when you're whoring, there are strategies involved.

Over the course of my career, I slept with many strippers, famous actresses, flight attendants, and even a porn star. When I slept with the porn star, I checked that off my bucket list.

I even fell in love with one stripper. I was in my early twenties and she was almost 40. She was a stripper that always came out and danced to Frank Sinatra songs. I used to call her "Frankie." That woman taught me many tricks.

In 2001 or 2002, my stripper train came to a screeching halt. I was finally taught a lesson when a stripper tried to extort money from me. I would see her regularly to party and have sex. This is when I was heavily into ecstasy. This stripper claimed I knocked her up and she threatened to tell my wife if I didn't pay her off.

She said if I gave her the cash she would move away and keep her mouth shut. I knew I was always "safe" sexually with her so I held her off until the child was born. My assistant at the time intervened and called bullshit. She told her she wasn't getting a dime and threatened her into having a paternity test. The kid wasn't mine, of course. It was fathered by her husband, who was in on the shakedown scam. I was done with strippers at that point. I burned myself out on that lifestyle.

Today, you can barely drag me into a strip club. It actually totally turns me off now.

Over the years I had a few long-term affairs. There was a bartender that I met at a Detroit-area establishment. We had an affair for several years. She eventually married a mutual acquaintance of my first wife and mine. We were ballsy during our affair. She attended parties and gatherings that my wife and I attended, even some at my home. My new wife and I have run into her recently. I told Sheryl who she was and about the affair we had and about how bold we were.

Sheryl said she wanted to punch her in the mouth for my ex-wife Cheryl's sake. It felt good to be able to be honest about her.

It baffles me to think how bold she and I were back then. I just didn't care. I'm ashamed now, but at the time it seemed exciting.

I had another long-term relationship with a woman that started during my Grinder days when I was still married. It was near the end of my marriage. I actually moved her in with me after my divorce from

Cheryl. She got into pills and alcohol deeply. Ironically, it was at a time when I wasn't abusing anything. I sent her to rehab and paid the $30,000 rehab program fee for her.

When I was signed to Calgary we ended our relationship. She came to visit in Calgary once. Then I met Anna, who became my second wife. When I would leave Anna in Calgary and come back to Michigan to visit family I would hook up with this woman time and time again. When I moved back in 2007 to Detroit she and I connected again until 2008.

She wanted to settle down and have kids. I wanted to party and be free. That's why I ended it for good.

It baffled me then, and still does today, that women act foolishly when it comes to being able to "spend time" with a pro athlete. Sheryl is the first woman that handles being with me and dealing with fans without showing fits of jealousy or anger.

Because of that, I've been able to be completely honest with her about my past.

She and I get a huge kick out of it most times and have good laughs about the actions and lengths some women go to reach out to me. But there is now a line that I have drawn. When the line is crossed, my wife softly reminds the "female fan" with a smile to simply "be respectful."

That usually works. It takes excessive behavior for Sheryl to even get to the point where she feels she has to say something. For example, there was a well-dressed woman in her early forties who came barreling through a crowd when I was signing autographs at a festival in Northern Michigan. This woman finally pushed through the crowd of people and reached me. She stood directly in front of me and grabbed my hand and started to push it down her pants, in front of Sheryl. I jerked my hand back when I realized what was happening and screamed, *"Get the fuck outta here!"*

Sheryl looked the woman in the eyes and said, "You should be embarrassed, that's pathetic, stop being desperate, get some class."

There was another incident when we were at a local bar during a holiday weekend and I was signing autographs. Keep in mind, my wife is not a drinker. Still, I drag her with me everywhere because I feel like she's my security blanket. People were coming up to me getting photographs and autographs. The bar was busy and the crowd situation became chaotic. My two friends were handling it. But a woman in her early twenties kept coming up to me and literally dry humping my leg. Whispering in my ear, she was begging me to take her with me. She was telling me over and over the things she wanted to do to me. It was the strangest situation ever. We'd pull her off of me and she'd push through the crowd and grab me again. She continued to gyrate on my leg like a dog in heat. The dirty talk also continued. I pointed to Sheryl (who was only my girlfriend at the time) and told the crazy girl that Sheryl was my wife and that she would kill her if she didn't go away.

She replied, "Fuck your wife, I don't care!"

I pushed her off my leg and my guy friends grabbed her and put her back into the crowd. Even her friends would come and fetch her. But in a flash she'd be back. I kept motioning for Sheryl, who was sitting a few feet away, to come deal with her because she clearly wasn't listening to my guy friends.

Sheryl would just look over and point and laugh, not realizing how serious the situation was becoming, Sheryl would wink and blow kisses just to be a smart ass.

Finally, about the fifth or sixth time this girl came back, she almost knocked me over along with a few patient fans who had waited respectfully, and I told her to get away from me.

However, this time I bellowed it loudly and pushed her off my leg. She came right back like a magnet, forcing her crotch into my leg. Sheryl heard me and realized that I was serious. I turned around and grabbed Sheryl and said, "Either you take care of this crazy bitch or I'm going to!"

Sheryl pulled the woman off my leg and said, "Sweety, be respectful, people are waiting to meet Darren and you're embarrassing yourself. Just be respectful."

The crazy woman screamed, "Fuck you!" right in Sheryl's face. Sheryl smiled at her and told her, "Last warning, go away and don't come back. You've had your time, leave him alone."

The woman's friends saw the commotion again and grabbed her and took her away. Literally within 20 seconds the girl came raging back and straight to my leg. The next thing I knew my buddy said "Darren turn around—LOOK!"

I turned around and saw that Sheryl, who stands 6', had this woman up in the air off her feet by her throat and literally threw her across the bar. She went flying, knocking down tables and chairs and people. Sheryl cleared the bar like a bowling ball knocking down pins. It was like Moses parting the Red Sea.

The woman's male friend ran up to Sheryl and grabbed her. I spun around as Sheryl was mid-swing, and grabbed her arm before her fist made contact with his face. I grabbed him by his neck. The bouncers and owner (who is a friend of mine) came and intervened and threw him out. I instructed the owner to throw the girl out too, and that's exactly what they did.

Some people have no limits. Some treat me like I'm public property—especially women. It always annoyed me, but at times I'd take advantage of the situation if it involved a really hot crazy chick. Now that I am a committed man, though, it really pisses me off.

A lady in her late fifties walked by me at a restaurant as I was eating dinner and grabbed a hold of my hair—she literally grabbed a handful and just jerked it. After she jerked my head back she smiled and walked away. Without saying a word, Sheryl got up and walked over to the lady and grabbed her by her arm and made her come apologize to me. She told the lady either she was going to walk over and apologize for grabbing my hair or she was going to get dragged over by *her* hair to apologize. She explained that I am not public property. The lady apologized and Sheryl let her go.

What annoys me the most though are the wasted fans that come up to me slobbering drunk at bars to tell me (slurring, drooling, and spitting) how I shouldn't drink alcohol or that they don't like that I drink in public. Yes friends, this really happens. The irony is staggering.

While I ponder my bad behavior through the years, I also wonder why women bought what I had to offer. It will always baffle me how these women somehow found a way to convince themselves that they were

213

going to be in a relationship with me, or that they were special, or that we were soul mates.

The reality was that I had a difficult time remembering their names, or juggling how to keep them low-key. Often, my mission was to figure out how to get rid of them. My favorite line was: "You're too good for me, I can't bring you into this crazy life of mine. It's not fair to you." That one worked well because it still made them feel like they had some worth to me and that it was me with the problem. None of them ever wanted to believe they had a problem, too.

I'm not saying that was an honorable way to end an affair. I'm saying that was a method that worked. It was a proven exit strategy.

I never understood why they kept coming back, even though the women knew I was married and knew, in their hearts, that they were being used for sex. They knew I wouldn't acknowledge my relationship with them to anyone. Yet they kept coming back.

When I read about Tiger Woods' exploits, I thought of my own lifestyle. I invested nothing in these relationships I had with multiple women, yet they imagined that they were in these deep loving relationships with me. Some of them clearly believed that we were going to be together forever when in reality it was just about sex to me.

There is no statute of limitations on how long a woman will believe she was still a special person in your life, even though you viewed her as a short-term dalliance.

In April 2013, I heard from a woman who I'd had an affair with around 2000 or 2001. She said she was waiting to hear from me because she always felt we were soul mates. She knew I was married back then, and she knew I was re-married now. She even knew my wife's name. But that didn't stop her from trying to rekindle our relationship.

In the midst of writing this book, a mistress from the 1990s reached out to me via email. What they don't know is that my email goes to my smartphone and to my wife's smartphone. We read them and laugh. Then I push delete. I rarely reply. The only time I do is if Sheryl knows and thinks I should because the woman won't stop emailing. In that case, I simply ask her to not contact me further.

Sheryl just shakes her head. "Baby, you're an awesome guy and all," she says. "But geez, you're not that amazing. These poor, desperate women."

As you will read, these people aren't always harmless. Your past comes back to bite you. Sometimes it bites the people you love. Those wounds sting the most.

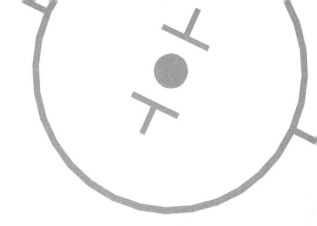

Chapter 17

The Last Dance

"I'm doin' the best I ever did, I'm doin' the best that
I can, I'm doin' the best I ever did, now go away"

—"Whatever"
Godsmack

The Last Dance

"I bless those who curse me and pray for those who have spitefully used me. I am sorry, I had to leave them behind."

—Hulk Hogan

Everyone wants to be friends with Darren McCarty, the former Detroit Red Wings hero, and no one wants to be friends with Darren the addict.

The oddity of my situation is that fans always want to be around me, while others who have been close to me in the past now want nothing to do with me. Fans want to shake my hand and talk about the Stanley Cup wins, while some of my former friends and family members have shut me out of their lives.

Some say they can't be around me because I drink, but I wonder if they would be more tolerant of my drinking if I still had a million dollars in my bank account.

Right or wrong, my take is that if you are with me when I'm holding the Stanley Cup over my head, then you should also be with me when I'm just scraping money together to pay my bills.

It's devastating to me that I seem to be ex-communicated from some friends and family members. I'm sure they would argue that it's a "tough love" approach, something they learned from Al-Anon. Maybe to them, it seems like the right way to deal with the situation. But from my perspective, it feels like betrayal.

During this book process, I went to see one of my friends, Sean "X-Pac" Waltman, once a champion WWE wrestler. He was at a small gig in Ybor City, Florida, when I saw him. He has battled drug and alcohol problems, and his best earning years are well behind him. But I was introduced to his mother, who was there supporting him even after his fall from stardom. He told me his mother has always stood beside him through his multiple incidents with substance abuse and rehab stints. Today, Sean is making his comeback. He has conquered many demons in his life; I hope he never stops fighting too.

When I heard that story I had to excuse myself to go to the bathroom because I was holding back tears. I stood there at the sink and splashed cold water on my face. It took me several minutes to pull myself back together.

I often think about my late stepfather, Craig. I feel as if I would still be close to my family if he were still alive. I don't think he would have allowed the situation to deteriorate as much as it has. His death changed my life in so many ways. My grandfather and Craig were the two father figures I had in my life, and both left this world far too early.

Those were the two men in my life who could hold me accountable. They were the two men who could guide me toward the right line of thinking. When Craig died I was left with only women trying to tell me what to do. I needed a male role model to help me through my issues.

Today, I fill some of the voids in my life through my new relationships with Sheryl's family. My mother-in-law is a beautiful woman who holds bible studies in an after-school program and preaches at the jail once a week. She prays for me and texts me messages of encouragement. My stepmother-in-law and father-in-law have also helped me. Sheryl's dad is an alcoholic, and he overcame his addiction to become successful in business. He went from poverty to wealth and back again a few times before finding long-term sobriety. He has been sober for more than 30 years. He's an inspiration.

A person doesn't know me just because he or she knows my NHL statistics. You can't learn anything about me as a person by reviewing my numbers.

If you want to know what I'm about, look at my ink work. My tattoos say more about me than my goal total does.

In 2008, *Inked Magazine*, the *Sports Illustrated* for tattoo aficionados, listed me as one of its All-Stars for being one of the professional athletes with the most intriguing etchings on his body.

Tattoos are forms of self-expression, like songs or poetry or paintings. You probably won't be shocked to know that I was with Bob Probert when I received my first body art work in 1994. I paid the artist to do an Aries with an "HD" (for Harley-Davidson) running through it. That was representative of my life at that time.

But my other tattoos are far more personal. You don't want to be saluted on my left arm because that's my tribute arm. You could say I wear my heart on my sleeve. That's where I have a cross and chain as a tribute to my stepdad, Craig, and my grandfather, Jigs. That's also where I pay homage to my musician friend, James Anders. His design has the words, "It's all about rock."

My right arm is my legacy arm. That's where I have an artist-rendition of a Griffin, a menacing four-footed medieval beast. That's to commemorate the birth of my son, who is named Griffin.

You're probably wondering why there are no tattoos on my body commemorating my four Stanley Cup championships. That's because those titles, as proud as I am of winning them, do not represent who I am as a human being.

Someday, my intention is to complete the vine on my right arm to include ivy and birth flowers to celebrate the birth of my daughters. I still want to add some paws on my left arm to pay tribute to some beloved family pets. I would also like to have a tattoo of my grandmother's cherry oak piano. I still need to have these additions designed though. (I'd like to get a tattoo that's a tribute to Sheryl, but she won't let me because she says it's bad luck for a relationship. It's an old Italian wives' tale that if you tattoo a tribute to a lover on your body it curses the relationship, but I'm still trying to talk her in to it.)

If you want to get to know me, just study my tattoos. My life is all there in my ink. I've wanted new tattoos for a while, but can't seem to get it done. My tattoo work remains a work in progress, much like my life.

Although I'd hoped to have a more normal life when I cleared away the troublesome people in my life, it didn't end all of the drama.

The initial thought that everyone had when I began making changes in my life was that Sheryl had come in and demanded that I do it. The truth is that Sheryl didn't demand I do anything. I was ready to change. I wanted to clear my trees and start a new life with Sheryl. That wasn't something she made me do. It was something I longed to do. It was exhausting mentally and physically to live the wild life I was living. Even though I was surrounded by people, it was a lonely existence because I knew none of those people were in my life long-term.

But the deadbeats I trimmed from life decided to blame Sheryl for the "new" me. Two waitresses I'd been dating even worked together to launch a hateful slander campaign against Sheryl and me.

When I was dating these women, they all hated each other. But as soon as I ended things they all started hating me because I wanted nothing to do with them.

They posted a nasty message on the "97.1 The Ticket" Facebook page when it was announced that I was going to be working there as a sports talk-show host.

When Borders announced that I was going to be sitting with Dani Probert to sign Bob's book, these people attacked me on Borders' website.

The lies they spread about me caused great harm to my reputation. They told people that I was selling crack out of my basement, a lie that even reached people within the Detroit Red Wings organization. Of course, I wasn't selling drugs. The truth is that I didn't even have a basement.

They were just angry that they were no longer associated with a former Detroit Red Wings player.

Sheryl made the mistake of trying to fight back, and their actions became even more hurtful. Then we tried to ignore them, but that also didn't work. At one point, someone from my former group wrote a letter to the hospital where Sheryl worked and said she was stealing drugs so I could sell them.

Fortunately, the hospital administrator laughed that one off because Sheryl's drug counts had never been off during her time at the hospital.

Plus, these nitwits posted their letter-writing plan on Facebook and we were able to point people to their Facebook page and show them what these women were capable of doing. We were not dealing with people of superior intelligence.

In July, Sheryl was accused of breaking the window in a car belonging to one of the women. We were able to prove Sheryl wasn't even in town at the time.

We routinely received threatening messages from them, usually around 3:00 AM, after the bars had closed. The situation was well beyond out of hand, but they took it to a new level when a friend showed us a conversation on their Facebook page. They said Sheryl needed to be "taken care of" because this chick's window had been broken and they said it was Sheryl who had broken it.

For me, that was the last straw. I felt like we had to do something to protect ourselves.

Armed with copies of the Facebook postings and text messages, we went to the police department and filed charges. We were advised to also seek a Personal Protection Order (PPO).

The judge granted us an immediate PPO ex parte, meaning it was granted without the other parties being present for a hearing. Judges don't like to grant ex parte orders because they seem to be in conflict with the spirit of the fifth and 14th amendments, which assure that people are entitled to due process in court proceedings.

But judges will grant ex parte orders if there is overwhelming evidence, which we presented.

In the granting of the PPO, the judge warned us to be careful. Of course, the media reported on the legal proceedings and one of the women hired a lawyer to fight the PPO.

It quickly became a media event. Sheryl and I became headlines. The story was picked up by every newspaper, website, and television station. We had the television people knocking at our door. Media attention has been part of my life for many years; I can roll with the punches. Sheryl, however, was freaked out by the attention. It doesn't make sense to her that we were victimized in this situation *and* we were being hounded by the media.

As we drove to the court for the legal proceedings, our attorney warned us that every media outlet had asked for, and received, the judge's permission to document the proceedings.

That means that cameras seemed like they were in my wife's face as she was testifying in the case. We had been threatened and harassed and now we were being violated by the process.

The opposing counsel tried to present emails, supposedly from Sheryl, showing that we had made threats. But they were not from my wife's account, or from any email account my wife ever owned (In fact, Sheryl's name was even spelled wrong on the fake email account). The judge did not accept those as evidence.

But the circus-like atmosphere of the event convinced Sheryl that we were being more harmed than helped by our decision to use the legal system to provide protection.

"Darren, these people are insane," Sheryl said. "Plus, the piece of paper [PPO] isn't going to protect us anyway. Let's stop the media invasion into our lives, and let's not give these women and their attorneys any more fame."

She suggested that we offer to settle this if the women removed all of the hateful comments from the social media sites and agreed not to make any more public comments about us.

"Because we went through with this, the police have it all on our record that they have threatened us," Sheryl said.

That's the offer we made, and it was accepted. The agreement was that all of the posts had to be removed, and no further posts about us would be allowed. The judge only agreed to drop three of the four PPOs, though, keeping open temporarily the one for the woman who was involved in a Facebook conversation about my wife being "taken care of."

We had to go back to court 30 days later to resolve that issue.

After the final PPO was dropped, one attorney went to the media and was quoted saying, "It's unfortunate that athletes and their spouses believe they are entitled to special treatment even far long after they've been out of the spotlight." He went on to say, "Fortunately, for us in this case, in the courtroom justice was blind and ultimately the correct decision was made."

This was ironic because his client was the client that the judge initially kept the PPO active against for an additional 30 days. We made the decision to dismiss it, no one else. The judge's decision was never given in this case, except to continue this particular PPO for 30 days. We literally had to go back to have it dismissed. When we did, the judge kept asking us if we were sure that this was the decision we wanted to make.

It just goes to show that what the media reports and what actually happens are two very different things.

All of this is public record, so anyone who wants to review the records can. I'm glad of that because I have nothing to hide.

The public record shows that one of these ridiculous human beings said that my wife should be harmed because her window was bashed in.

In a Facebook conversation, one of her "friends" said he would do it so she wouldn't have to get her "hands dirty."

Another guy said he would come in his "death truck" and get it done for her.

The fascinating aspect of the situation is that the woman testified under oath that she never accused my wife of breaking her window, even though we presented the Facebook evidence.

Under oath, she also said that no one had broken her window. She said it had been broken by the summer heat.

This situation was created by sick, hateful, and delusional people. When I was going through this, all I could think about was how I spent all of my time with these kinds of people when I was in my dark period. I let these people in my life. It makes me sick to know that my poor choices a few years ago meant Sheryl had to go through this ordeal.

"It's okay, babe," Sheryl would say. "These people don't scare me."

She should have run the other way when she met me, or left my ass when she discovered how I was living in 2009. But she stayed with me, first as a friend and now as a wife. Her love has never wavered. I now understand what true love is about.

Sheryl saved my life.

When I pointed out that my mess with my 3:00 AM girlfriends is public record, it occurred to me that my life is essentially public record. Once I beat up Claude Lemieux, I was never again going to have a private life.

My employment history since I retired from the game is well known. I worked for Versus as an analyst until NBC Sports Network took over,

225

at which point my boss was fired, which meant that everyone he hired was fired. After that is when I worked in the pawn shop business with American Jewelry and Loan on Greenfield Road in Detroit. I was featured on the reality show *Hardcore Pawn*.

I'd gone in there in 2011 with a buddy who was trying to sell an alligator skin for $4,000 (he ended up getting $2,000). I'd always been interested in the pawn business, one thing led to another, and I found myself learning the business.

Anyone who watched the television show knows that it's a crazy business. One day a man came in and pawned his artificial leg, and then he came back a few days later and paid to get it back.

One of my favorite pawn-shop stories was shown on the television show. A kid came into the store trying to sell what he said were authentic Darren McCarty and Kris Draper jerseys.

Believe it or not, this was not set-up. This young man had no idea that I worked there, and the look on his face when I popped out was priceless.

He wanted way too much money, especially when we could see that he essentially had two jerseys that you could buy at the store for $100 each.

I took grief when I offered the kid $120 total for both jerseys. They insisted it was too much to pay.

"Yes," I said, "but I'm going to sign one and I'm going to get Kris Draper to sign the other and we are going to sell them for $250."

That's exactly what happened. We got $500 for the pair. I know how the autograph world works, especially now that I'm heavily dependent upon that world for income. I'm still popular enough with Detroit fans to make regular autograph appearances.

I also tried my hand as a sports talk-show host on The Ticket. During the Red Wings' 2013 playoff run I was a warm-up act for the pregame festivities. I came on and introduced a video of highlights from the past, and then I got people jacked up with the chant, "Let's go Wings!"

To be honest, I'm not sure what I want do with my life. Maltby, Osgood, Chris Chelios, and Draper all immediately joined the Red Wings organization in different capacities. I'm not sure if I'd be good at that kind of work, or happy in it; I've never been offered.

But what I really think I'm better suited for is media work. If you look around the media landscape, you see a lot of former NHL goalies and tough guys doing media work because we know the game inside-and-out, but I haven't been able to get that kind of work.

My friends and I always joke around that my dream job would be to succeed either Paul Woods or Mickey Redmond if they ever decide to retire from their positions as the Red Wings' radio and television analysts.

If there was ever someone who was born to earn his living talking about hockey, it was me. I certainly know the game and I already have a relationship with Detroit fans.

I believe I have a good perspective about what it means to be a Red Wing, and what it means to be an athlete in general. I think I have a much broader understanding of the bigger picture now that I'm retiring and trying to find my place in a changing world.

As this book was being written, America dealt with the tragic Boston Marathon bombing. The feelings I had were similar to what I felt on September 11, 2001, when terrorists took down the World Trade Center.

I was at Red Wings training camp in Traverse City, Michigan, taking part in a fitness test that I always called "30 seconds of hell," when the news came. This particular fitness test ends with an all-out sprint that leaves you huffing and puffing. I was bent over, trying to catch my breath, when the news came across the television that an airplane had struck one of the towers. Like the rest of America, I assumed it was a horrible, tragic accident involving air traffic control and/or instrument failure.

But when I caught my breath and looked up to see the second plane slamming into the tower my first thought was *Terrorism*.

That moment changed all of us. It made me remember that the world of sports isn't the life-and-death world that we act like it is. But sports have their place, even during a time of crisis.

The memory I have about the events of 9/11 was the sight of planes landing at the smallish Traverse City Airport. I remember counting 45 airplanes of all sizes parked nose-to-tail everywhere in the airport as airlines complied with the U.S. government's orders to get every plane out of the sky.

Training camp was temporarily postponed as America mourned her dead. When we resumed play and started playing games again, people seemed more appreciative of sports.

I realized then that athletes have an essential role in society's structure. We provide the entertainment that allows people to check out of their lives, at least temporarily. We provide the moments of escape from the scariness of the real world. We play a role in keeping the country's spirit's high. Yes, I know that athletes are paid too much—I wish we paid our police officers and teachers more. But athletes have a role in making us feel normal and alive.

Didn't you cry when you watched the Boston Red Sox ceremony after the Boston Marathon bombing in 2013? I certainly did.

The other lasting impact that 9/11 had on me was that it made me realize the value I place on being what I call a "Canamerican." I'm still a Canadian citizen, but I'm as much an American as I am a Canadian.

I care deeply about what happens in this country, and I'm proud of how everyone pulls together when there is a national crisis. When there is a problem, we stand shoulder-to-shoulder like it's us against the world. And it may not be far from the truth to say it *is* us against the world.

We put aside our geographic, cultural, or political differences when there is a national crisis. When the Boston Marathon is bombed, then we are all from Boston, even if we live in Michigan or New York or Florida. That's who we are. That's what being an American is all about. In Michigan, we might be either a Sparty or a Wolverine, and we can be at each other's throats during a football season. But a Sparty or a Wolverine would stand together for America. They can resume hating each other later.

America's protective instincts are very similar to the fighting culture in the NHL. We protect our own. We stand up for our teammates, whether we like them or not.

It's like the big brother who constantly pounds on his little brother—but if anyone else messed with his little brother, he would pound the shit out of him.

Since I'm now married to an American, I may even consider becoming an American citizen, although that will come after I decide what to do with my life. I would love to find a way to stay connected to the game of hockey.

I feel as if there is a plan for me, but I'm not sure yet what it is. Meanwhile, I'm still raging war against my alcohol addiction. It's a ferocious fight and there have been many casualties. My family can attest to that.

I am not a religious person, at least not in terms of embracing an organized religion. But I've always believed that I had a direct line to God. I've felt that way ever since I was young.

Many times in my life I've had a feeling that I was being guided to do one thing or another, and I've always felt like it was God steering me in the right direction.

That's why I feel that eventually I'm going to end up where I need to be. I'm going to find a job that I was meant to hold. I'm going to end up with people who want me to be with them.

I have faith that my life will eventually work out, as long as I continue to fight against my addiction. I know I can't give in because my disease has fatal consequences. That's why this is my last fight, and why it's the most important fight I have ever had.

Sometimes a casual Detroit Red Wings fan will stop me on the street, knowing that I'm a former player, someone they recognize but they can't quite put a name to my face.

"Aren't you Bob Probert?" they often ask.

"Bob is dead," I say. "I'm Darren McCarty, and I'm very much alive."

Epilogue

When I saw Brendan Shanahan the first time after *My Last Fight* was published, he said, "Thanks Darren, for forcing me to explain to my 11-year-old why I was stretching naked in my hotel room."

My teammates and I have shared more than a few laughs over some of the stories I chose to use in my book.

The publicity tour for my book in the fall of 2013 was happening around the time the NFL's Miami Dolphins suspended lineman Richie Incognito for his alleged verbal harassment and racist remarks directed at teammate Jonathan Martin. I remember telling fans that an incident of that nature would never happen in an NHL dressing room.

I hope it was clear in this book that in Detroit we loved each other off the ice as much as we did on the ice. That's one reason why we won as often as we did.

One of my goals in writing this book was to make it 75 percent about life and 25 percent about hockey because I wanted even non-hockey fans to be able to relate to what I was talking about.

Although I don't know what the final breakdown was, I believe we ended up with the proper ratio because I've talked to many people who don't know hockey, who still enjoyed the book.

One fan told me: "I couldn't get through Bobby Orr's book because it was too much about hockey. I liked your book because it was about you as a person."

Many people have come up to me to say they could relate to what I was going through because they had gone through bankruptcy, divorce, alcoholism, or drug addiction, or all of the above.

Some of the letters I received were heartbreaking, particularly one from a mother whose son, a Red Wings fan, had died. She had buried him in one of my jerseys. I couldn't even finish the letter.

Another one of my book goals, or maybe I should call it a hope, was that a young NHL prospect in the Canadian Hockey League or college could read my book and I think, *I need to avoid the fucking mistakes that Darren McCarty made.*

If you read the book, you know that I laid out the path that you shouldn't follow. I've been there, done that, paid the consequences, and now you don't have to go there. Lessons can be learned as much from stories of where other people go wrong in their lives.

Just from all of the people I've met since the book came out, I know there was enough humor in the book to keep everyone reading. People have told me that they had no idea how funny goalie Kevin Hodson was.

When I went to the Bob Probert memorial motorcycle ride for charity in 2014, I ran into Ryan Vandenbussche, who said immediately: "So you got tired of hitting me, eh?"

We shared some laughs about my stories of not wanting to fight him because he would never quit. I would become worn out hitting him so many times. He told me that former Cornwall coach Marc Crawford had told him to go after me. Remember, I was a big scorer in junior hockey.

I told everyone at Probert's motorcycle event that if they didn't like anything in the book they should "just blame it on Bobby," because he wrote his book first and I was just following his lead.

"Plus," I said, "don't we blame Bobby for everything?"

A year after my book-writing experience I still haven't decided for sure what I want to accomplish with the rest of my life.

What I have committed to is becoming healthy again. Accidentally setting myself on fire changed my life.

In April 2014, I had a fire pit roaring, burning cedar wood in my backyard. The grass had been cut that day, and some of the gas from the lawnmower had spilled onto the grass. Cedar creates large ash, and it was a windy day. The ash blew onto the yard, igniting the grass and some hedge clippings that I had trimmed earlier in the day near the garage.

Spotting the fire, I wasn't the least bit concerned. My plan was to walk over and stomp it out.

By the time I had taken three steps, the fire spread across the grass and my track-suit pants were engulfed in flames. One of my sneakers melted from the heat. You could smell the rubber burning

Immediately, I kicked off my shoes, pulled off my socks, and stripped down to my boxers.

Just then I saw the fire spreading toward the garage, where we keep the gasoline and the snow blower and other gas-powered items. Making a dash for the hose, I was able to extinguish the flames before the garage blew up or was set ablaze. However, my leg was burned. Still, I wasn't overly concerned.

"You're a nurse," I told Sheryl. "Bandage me up."

But the skin was already peeling off my legs, so she immediately took me to Beaumont Hospital, where the doctors realized that I had second- and third-degree burns. They decided to send me to the specialist at DMC Hospital.

As it turned out, I was fortunate not to need skin grafts.

For three weeks, I couldn't stand up. And I went more than two months without putting on a shoe. After about eight weeks, I was back golfing, but I had to wear flip-flops. It actually improved my golf game because I've had to slow down my swing.

During all my doctor visits, my lab work made it clear to doctors and Sheryl that I had to stop drinking or else. I think we all know what the "or else" is. You can't drink excessively for years and not pay a price for that.

Won't say I've been perfect, but I'm moving in that direction. My medical issues have finally grabbed my attention and I've been able to stay sober.

When I was still drinking, Sheryl did all of the driving. I don't climb behind the wheel when I'm drinking. If I take one drink, Sheryl has the keys. I've been good about that. She has had to make an adjustment to not being my chauffer because I'm driving again. I just drove 18 of the hours of the trip from Michigan to Florida.

It feels as if I'm more focused on avoiding alcohol. I spend my days scheduling time for Sheryl, fishing, golf, and darts. I'm a retired player, and right now I'm enjoying what retired people do. I'm content to wait and see what tomorrow will bring.

—Darren McCarty
July 2014